MAKING GOSPEL SENSE

Making Gospel Sense
To a Troubled Church

James Wm. McClendon, Jr.

The Pilgrim Press

Cleveland, Ohio

The Pilgrim Press, Cleveland, Ohio 44115
© 1995 by James Wm. McClendon, Jr.

Biblical quotations not otherwise marked are from the Revised English Bible (REB) ©
Oxford University and Cambridge University Presses 1989, and are used by permission;
others as marked are from the New Revised Standard Version (NRSV), Today's English
Version (TEV), King James Version (KJV), or Cotton Patch Version (CPV).

00   99   98   97   96   95   5   4   3   2   1

Library of Congress Cataloging-in-Publication Data
McClendon, James William.
Making Gospel sense : to a troubled church / James Wm. McClendon, Jr.
p.   cm.
Includes bibliographical references and index.
ISBN 0-8298-1072-2 (alk. paper)
1. Sermons, American. I. Title.
BV4253.M3614   1995
252—dc20
95-180872
CIP
Rev.

To Michael Goldberg

CONTENTS

INTRODUCTION

Envision a small, struggling church almost devoid of children and youth. Picture dissension between leading members and other leading members. Frame a sequence of pastoral disasters stretching over several years' time—resignations, ministerial firings, assorted failures in leadership and its skills. Suppose that what remains is a discouraged congregation whose attendance on a good Sunday is forty or less. Forty or fewer bodies—each wanting and needing to be *some*body, none quite able to discern *the* body that is the body of Christ that is the church. And yet none (or hardly any) quite ready to abandon this congregation, either, none disposed to deny that Christ is in its midst or that this church can live. Close to shared despair, barely able to function, yet not willing to die, here is a church in a particular sort of trouble.

To be true to itself, the church needs to be in trouble. The ancient name of that trouble is the cross. When Jesus instructs the disciples that they are to take up their cross and follow him (Mark 8:34 and par.), he locates his church on earth in a state of adversity that must last while the world lasts. The cross is not to be our lot forever, but it is ours today and likely tomorrow. To put the point in less traditional terms, only a community whose ongoing social nonconformity evokes sure opposition from a faithless world can be the present church of Jesus Christ. The gospel message to such Christian communities in cruciform trouble is that they are in the right place at the right time.

Yet churches may also find themselves in other sorts of trouble.

These troubles come not from following Jesus but from avoiding or missing his way. There is the trouble of disciples who turn aside to squabble with one another while their master heads for Jerusalem (see Mark 9:33–37). There are introverted communities that segregate themselves from outsiders for what they consider good reasons (see Acts 10). There is the confusion that comes from false doctrine (see 2 Thess. 2:1f.). And there are still other troubles that cannot be equated with taking up the cross.

It is not the purpose of these pages to canvass every sort of trouble into which the saints can stray. It seems more helpful to stick to one concrete case—the very case that evoked the sermons reproduced here. Where can such troubled churches as this be found? Statistics on American church life suggest that they exist almost everywhere: in inner cities, occupying great, moldering buildings; in aging suburban sanctuaries avoided by the upwardly mobile; of course, in depopulated open country locations. Reports indicate that the *average* congregation in America consists of about forty worshipers, far short of the fantasies of ambitious young preachers. One finds these wilting churches everywhere—often the residue of great dreams, sometimes the harvest of decades of hard work, not seldom the aftermath of high-minded mission adventures gone awry. They have not quite succeeded as churches (have not quite found their way to the true trouble?), but after all is said and done they have not quite failed, either. To say the least, their hurting is not counterfeit pain.

Sometimes such churches need to die. Their positive energies are better dispersed into other, existing congregations, or even into a new congregation that rises, phoenixlike, from the ashes of the old. Some denominations offer programs to achieve such transitions: With appropriate ceremony an old church is closed and a new one commissioned in its place. The old congregation is dismissed and with it the problems it could never resolve. A new congregation, it is reckoned, has a better chance of life. Of course, spiritual judgment is required to discern the cases where such a formal closure is in order.

Will the desired resurrection in fact follow? When Matthew's Jesus said of his projected fellowship that "the doors of death will not hold out against it" (Matt. 16:18 CPV), he was not, as I understand that text, promising eternal deathlessness to the first disciple band or to any later church or communion. The military image in this text is not one of defense but of attack: The defenses erected against the gospel by the realm of death (its "gates" or "doors") will not withstand the power of the coming Rule of God, power that Jesus says will inhere in his church. Which is to say that while a troubled congregation is in no sense immortal, yet if it be indeed a church, it trembles with an irresistible energy to overcome troubles and regain its mission. If that energy is present, it may not be wise to let a troubled church die.

Others have written, and written well, about the strategies of organization, enlistment, structural change, and management available to small churches with their troubled hopes. (See, for example, David R. Ray, *The Big Small Church Book*, and the earlier collection edited by Jackson W. Carroll, *Small Churches Are Beautiful*.*) These strategies and skills are not what this book is about.

What, then, is it about? At the center of authentic Christian community stand certain great gospel signs. Most Christian confessional documents say something about baptism and Lord's supper, and something as well about prophetic preaching. In some theologies, some or all of these practices are called sacraments; in other theologies they are called ordinances. In my own thinking, baptism, eucharist, and preaching are together understood as evangelical *signs*. (In Scripture, the term *sign* has a distinctive role—see for example *sēmeion* in the Gospel of John.) This book is about the sign of gospel preaching; it seeks to display and thus to focus anew its role among the great biblical signs.

I do not thereby deny or reject the strategies of organization and

---

*These and other books are included in a short Booklist at the end of this book; there readers may find data on books of interest mentioned in these pages.

renewal offered by the technique books. In particular cases they may be indispensable. Often we could make no headway in church recovery without something like them. Yet there is something more central than they, something proved by longer use than they, more biblical than they, more evangelical than any of them. This is the faithful, continual employment of the God-given, gospel signs. Among these, *prophetic preaching*, biblically rooted, dynamic, demanding, has its inalienable place.

Such are my convictions. They may be ones that my reader shares. Yet what a gap there is for us between profession and practice! Read on.

By choice my wife and I were members of a small church in a middle-sized city, a northerly satellite of megalopolis Los Angeles, California. In that satellite city she and I lived and taught. (She teaches philosophy to seminarians; I, theology.) It had not come strongly home to us when we joined that the congregation we chose was already in trouble; we only noticed lovely, rather shy people, sharing a religious heritage close to our own, and seemingly faced with favorable prospects. We took our places quietly in that congregation, avoiding as much as possible committee assignments and leadership posts, for both of us were hard-pressed theological professionals. Symptoms of the coming furor were undoubtedly visible when we came, but we were slow to take alarm.

Then the trouble broke out. One week there was controversy, another week there was deep dissension involving key leaders; next, on a Sunday morning we learned that a board of the congregation duly empowered had dismissed the pastor. Some members appeared satisfied; others were distressed. The whole church was at odds. Its hopes had been staked upon this latest pastor, bringing him in from the Midwest, settling his family in the parsonage, and trusting his training to find the directions that would turn our congregation from decline to recovery. Some said this turnabout was an old story for this church, said that abrupt dismissals and sudden departures had occurred before. Others said the church had been wrongfully misled in its search process: this pastor had disappointed previous congregations in similar ways. And what, we inquired, was this latest pastor said to have done or failed to do? So far, little was clear. Certainly mutual trust between pastor and other leaders had disappeared. Later disclosure of the provoking events (a church member's quarrel with the departed pastor; his failure to provide needed organizational leadership or neglect of visitation) made them seem only symptomatic of the deeper troubles that infected our little band.

I will not list here the underlying ills that eventually surfaced; each is addressed more than once in the sermons that follow. It is enough to say that a church planted in Southern California late in the previous century by folk moving west from Pennsylvania, Ohio, and Indiana (its denominational heartland) had flourished for a while in a downtown California setting, had moved to the suburbs in the 1950s, in the sixties and seventies had gathered a sizable congregation and Sunday school and nurtured a new generation into faith—only to see its flock disperse, move away to other places, or simply drop out, leaving behind an aging and diminishing remnant of the faithful. Good singers, the remnant were, good church dinner cooks, good Christians, but Christians ill-trained for the tasks that next confronted them and ill-prepared for a series of misfortunes— including the most recent pastoral crisis.

Where to turn, what to do, how to recover? Money was not the urgent problem; the church building, though superficially damaged by a recent earthquake, was secure enough. People, missing people: that was the visible problem. Where were those who would fill the vacant pews, the leaders who would take places in the aging ranks? And beneath that highly visible need, where were the skills of heart to reunite a congregation disheartened by recent discouragements? There were not a few who said it was time to close the church, sell the building, disband. Resentment—of the ex-pastor, of one another—ran deep. The rancor reminded me of an old saying from the American West: What is the difference between wild horses and wild asses? When danger threatens the herd, wild horses gather in a circle, heads together, and kick out against the common foe. In similar circumstances, wild asses (so goes the saying) gather in a circle, heads out, put their hind quarters together—and kick each other!

This relation of facts may be tolerably objective, although in any church fuss, not everyone will agree about what has happened. I have at least reported my own initial perception of what went on in one troubled church. As I saw it then, it was, after all, others' trouble, not really mine. To be sure, if the church collapsed, my wife and I would need a new place of Bible study and worship and service to human need. Nothing more.

Now, though, came the catch. After two or three weeks in which the leadership tried other pulpit arrangements, they asked me to preach for a Sunday or two, and then asked if I would become the interim pastor. Suddenly the troubles noted by a friendly but detached observer became troubles to face each Sunday as preacher for Christ's flock. Thereby, a theological theory about baptism and eucharist and the word confronted me as uncompromising weekly duties. Without seeking the job, without much experience in this place, and rather late in my life's journey (it was in the course of my seventieth year), I was asked to take a place I had for years left to others.

I was not totally without experience. In the beginnings of my ministry, I had served two Baptist churches in Louisiana as pastor, one small, one considerably larger, and once a downtown church in Sydney, Australia, had made me interim pastor for half a year. But that was long ago. I had also served a number of ordinary California churches that in the normal course of things had seen an old pastor depart and were searching for or awaited the coming of a new one. These pleasant duties were also long past. Lately, living in a new place, even Sunday supply preaching had been only an occasional opportunity for me, and I had concentrated on a professor's tasks— teaching students who were getting ready for ministry (I even offered some advanced seminars in preaching!), mentoring doctoral students, and writing groundbreaking volumes of systematic theology. I had just submitted the latest of these, five hundred hard-crafted pages called *Doctrine,* to the publisher.

I was tired, I was old, and I had my share of self-doubt. Was it possible for a head-in-the-clouds seminary professor, no matter what he had been or done, to face the weekly demands of a church in trouble? The pastoral ministry had changed greatly since my own ministry began. The current demand in Southern California seemed to be for a churchly entertainer, a rival to the television talk show maestro, with a pulpit for a stage and a congregation as an audience. To be sure, the departed pastor of our congregation had not provided such a stage show, but then, his ministry was counted a failure, was it not? And even if the image of ministry was shaped not by Holly-wood but by the holy wood of Jesus' cross, even if the strategy of evangelism and nurture was determined not by Madison Avenue but by the presence of the Risen One—even then, could a gossamer theoretician still make it in the give-and-take of weekly ministry? I who for years had attended to theoretical statements of Christian faith, not to its everyday operations? And was the task not rather like persuading a herd of wild horses to give up behaving like a herd of wild asses?

There was another factor: The invitation to take up the pastoral duties made more plain my own (equine or asinine) involvement. For better or worse this church was now my own family's congregation. If it finally collapsed, there were, of course, other churches in town. That was a thought that doubtless occurred in our household as it did in others, though my wife and I never so much as mentioned it to one another. Yet if I agreed to serve as pastor-for-the-interim and if that interim ended in collapse, if, to use an old navy idiom, the ship went hard aground on my watch, leaving the church would not merely be acceding to a Providence that does after all allow some churches to die; it would also require reckoning with fresh personal failure. And even success would put a strain on my working wife, who in the course of our marriage had never before had to become Mrs. Interim Pastor. Since giving up a task once begun does not come easily in our family, I could most surely avoid all these hazards by refusing the call—which would be another sort of giving up. What should I do?

Fearing much, yet hoping too, I accepted the call.

The following pages are a record of sermons preached in the year's work that followed. They reach from the summer (and Pentecost season) in which my interim ministry began to the new summer (and new Pentecost season) in which it ended. Did I succeed? Of course the reader can turn to my closing report in this book and draw his or her own conclusions. Yet I prefer to recall matters in the order in which they took place. These sermons appear in the order of their preaching. There were indeed other, intervening sermons; I have only included enough here to represent the rest. On rare occasions I have heightened the rhetorical force of what is printed so that it can equal what I believe to have been the force of the spoken words, print not being so lively a medium as speech. Mostly, though, what stands here is what was said in one troubled church.

In choosing texts, usually yet not always I followed the guidelines of the denominational lectionary, and we tended to follow these readings in the Sunday liturgy as well, unfailingly reading both from Old Testament and New. I believe the sequence of the Christian year is a significant defense against the rhythms of secularity that throb in our California hearts. On the other hand, I did not hesitate to substitute a text when I believed it would better speak to our urgent need. In the free churches we have both the liberty to follow a regular lectionary and the liberty to depart from it when there is sufficient need.

For readers who preach or want to preach, a few words here about sermon preparation may be helpful. My practice is to begin with a text I believe will speak to the congregation in its present time and place, so that finding that text is the first task, one I ordinarily undertake on Sunday night or Monday morning. This allows only a week for its development. Thus my habit strikes a compromise between relevance (what do people need *now*?) and fidelity to the text (which might require much longer thought). Even when the text comes straight from a lectionary, this task of selection remains, as few if any Sunday lections provide as such unified sermon texts. What in Scripture is the word of God for this congregation this coming Sunday? *That* is the first sermonic question and in a way the last.

Once the text is chosen, my own principles of sermon construction are easily stated: I try to start where people are, start with what I think they already know or think. That yields an introduction. I try to follow that with some central picture or idea (perhaps a narrative image) that will help listeners discover for themselves the message I find in the text, the sermon's point. My hope is that such an image will be strong enough, clear enough, to make the sermon's central point clear to any listener, whether or not the rest of the sermon is heard. (As one who daydreams plenty during others' sermons, I am not critical of hearers who fail to follow every sentence.) Finally, I try to end the sermon on a strong downbeat, with substantial rhetorical energy. I do not always succeed at this last, and indeed I think that sermon conclusions, the great strength of the previous century's preaching, are our great weakness. Most of us present-day preachers start well, but we do not end well, and I am as deserving of that criticism as any. Yet I try.

There is a fresh narrative element in the best contemporary preaching, and I, too, look for narrative texts and narrative illustrations, with narrative playing against narrative so that for listeners "this is that" (Acts 2:16 KJV), the story then illuminating the story now, *becoming* the story now in hearers' understanding. When that happens, the word preached has become the word of God.

Readers who know that I am a working theologian may wonder where theology, that is, Christian ethics and Christian doctrine, fit into the sermon-building task. Well, theology is about Christian convictions—their discovery, their understanding, their reformulation in light of all God's truth. Not to share those convictions is not to be a Christian at all, much less a Christian preacher. Not to understand them in some measure disqualifies any man or woman as a teacher in Christ's church. And not to reformulate is to be a preacher who remains in some other time and place, not this time and place. So the preacher is constantly and of necessity about the theological task. Only it must be carried on as the first-order task of the teaching church, not as the second-order, more abstract, more abstruse work of the schools. Thus one must strike out of pulpit discourse terms of art ("hermeneutics," *prosopōn*, "foundationalism," and the like) that have a proper place in the lecture hall. And even the stalwart skeletal convictions of Christian theology (the deity of Christ, the universality of sin, the ecumenicity of holy community) must find their way into sermons only when clothed in the sinew and lean muscle (and sometimes even a little of the fat!) of a living body of discourse.

I have tried to publish these sermons pretty much as they were actually preached. That raises some typographical difficulties. The texts were not read aloud by the preacher if they were part of the regular reading of Scripture earlier in the service. Yet I print them here so that readers may connect with them without having to look each one up. Where it seems very important, I refer [in brackets, thus] to the readings that were not the text proper, but were important both to the service and to the sermon. To distinguish here the times that I mentioned an exact Scripture citation from the times that I only noted it in my manuscript for my own purposes, I will use the same device that I used in the pulpit: the former (the passages actually uttered) are in round parentheses; the latter [cited in my manuscript, but not read aloud] are in square brackets. The same rule applies to other uses of round and square brackets: they distinguish what I spoke aloud and what I did not.

Since both most of my readers and I know that the biblical God is neither male nor female nor some hermaphroditic combination of both, being truly a God beyond gender, it may surprise some that in these sermons I follow recent standard English versions of the Bible (including REB, NRSV, and others) in using generic "he" and "his" to refer to God in the biblical story. Is this inconsistent with my own belief? Some may think so, though there are sophisticated reasons to justify my use, but my actual reason is much simpler: what I did *included* more of my hearers than any alternative I knew. Perhaps what is most inclusive is still changing and will later be different; if so, slow change (the sort of change represented here) may take more of us along than lightning change can.

How are we to judge when the sermon has worked? It will not be enough to have gained listeners, not enough for vivid narrative or other imagery to appear, not enough for Christian convictions to lie beneath its surface, not enough though all the principles of rhetoric are fulfilled. These are necessary elements in preaching, but even when all are present they are insufficient. The supreme test is this: the sermon must come through as good news, as gospel. Addressing the actual sore spots in congregational life, for example, will be mere diagnosis, only a melancholy inventory of troubles, until to those troubles there comes a clear announcement of the grace of God in Jesus Christ: release to captive hearers, healing to sick hearers, good news to despairing hearers. To be sure, that good news will bring its own cruciform trouble with it. Yet this is the authentic gospel trouble, the trouble that means a cross to share, a troubling and troubled world to confront, good tidings not only to preach forth but to live out.

Sermons were not my only contribution to the interim year: I used the limited leverage of my office to make sure our small church followed patterns for baptism and eucharist that were consistent with its heritage (like other heirs of Radical Reform, we practiced believers baptism and held a semiannual Love Feast preceded by foot-washing). I also sought to make our patterns consistent with the great heritage of the church catholic—there is no conflict between these two goals. As an interim step, I insisted that the congregation progress to a monthly eucharist in place of the infrequent communion that had until recently prevailed. That gave tone to all the services, for it provided structure on which to build the remaining, noneucharistic Sunday liturgies, concluding these others each week with a grand offertory of prayers and gifts. (There is more on the theory involved here in chapter 9 of my volume *Doctrine*.)

I also fulfilled the emergency duties of a regular pastoral ministry. Happily, our fellowship had no funerals, and as it happened there were no weddings during my term. I did enlist Sunday school teachers, did organize an all-church workshop to clarify our future, did arrange a week of special services (we called it "Quest") for neighbors who were interested in learning to sing and pray and believe with us. I did visit prospective members and receive those who came in by transfer, and I attended more committee meetings than I had time to attend. Those who do these things regularly and easily might have laughed at my clumsiness in much of this.

Yet for better or worse, it was the great prophetic sign of gospel *preaching* that made the year what it was. If what follows is of use to readers, I am glad. In any case these sermons are useful to me, not because I will ever preach them again, but because in every one of them I preach first of all to myself.

Special thanks are due to the critical readers who at an early stage reviewed the manuscript and thus saved the author from a number of witless errors. They are Kyle and Jane Childress, Mitties De Champlain, and David Keyes. If these folk receive irate letters from subsequent readers, they should assume that the author stubbornly refused their good advice in those cases.

PART ONE

Grief and Forgiveness

(Five Sermons)

After the Funeral

From a leader in the small congregation where my wife and I were members came an anxious phone call: Relations between the pastor and some members, already tense and unhappy, had reached a breaking point: The pastor would not be present on Sunday; would I please preach? I accepted the invitation. I knew enough of what had happened to believe there was wrong on both sides, but I could see no way in which the situation could be reversed. What was God's word to this troubled situation?

The Christian response to division and enmity is forgiveness and reconciliation—the very work of Christ on earth. Yet there is a forgiveness too easily mouthed, a peace too insubstantial to matter. What was needed here, I thought, was a word from the pulpit that acknowledged the enmity and resentment burning on both sides in the church— acknowledged it and did not merely scold it or brush it aside as unworthy of good Christians—without either taking sides between those who had favored accepting the pastor's resignation and those who had not, or assigning blame to either or both.

Was there a biblical story that could illuminate our plight and also show the way toward restoration of our brittle and now splintering community? I thought of the Genesis portrayal of the enduring tension separating Joseph and his brothers, tension that broke out afresh upon the death of their father Jacob. In that story as in this there was a precipitating event (the death of Jacob; the departure of the pastor), and in both there was the reopening of old wounds. Our own story was far too fresh to be recited from the pulpit, but I could tell the Genesis story and count on listeners to see a parallel. Our plight would be acknowledged in a straightforward way, but it need not be magnified. Of course, the deeper appeal of this sermon is its movement toward forgiveness. However, as the old baptists, that is, the Anabaptists, knew, forgiveness a la Matthew 18 is a practice, not just an emotion.

Here, then, is the sermon I preached on short notice.

Now that their father was dead, Joseph's brothers were afraid, for they said, "What if Joseph should bear a grudge against us and pay us back for all the harm we did to him?" They therefore sent a messenger to Joseph to say, "In his last words to us before he died, your father gave us this message: 'Say this to Joseph: I ask you to forgive your brothers' crime and wickedness; I know they did you harm.' So now we beg you: forgive our crime, for we are servants of your father's God." Joseph was moved to tears by their words. His brothers approached and bowed to the ground before him. "We are your slaves," they said. But Joseph replied, "Do not be afraid. Am I in the place of God? You meant to do me harm; but God meant to bring good out of it by preserving the lives of many people, as we see today. Do not be afraid. I shall provide for you and your dependents." Thus he comforted them and set their minds at rest.   (Gen. 50:15–21)

The final chapter of the book of Genesis contains the story of an ancient funeral. I will not pretend to tell you about that funeral, for I am not well informed about funeral customs, ancient or modern. I mean instead to speak to you about something that both you and I do know about. And this is about how people feel and act when a sad thing has happened in the family. We know about this, even if we are not Jews. We know about it, even if we are not Christians. In such a case, we must not pretend that no sad thing has happened in our midst. In fact, a sad thing has happened to us in this church. Perhaps, like death, what happened was inevitable. But when someone dies, we do not simply shrug and say, "Oh, well, everybody dies." That is not a human response to such a loss. No, our reaction is to grieve, and like it or not, we are a grieving congregation today. Our guests must respect our grief; they cannot share it as we do, but they cannot fail to see it, either.

The question is, what happens after the grief, *after the funeral?* That is the part of the Genesis story that I do want you to consider. You remember the longer story. Joseph, younger son born to old

Jacob in the Land of Promise, had been hated and resented by his older brothers. When Judah and Simeon and Reuben and all the eleven saw a chance, they had kidnapped their younger brother, sold him to slave traders bound for Egypt, and poured blood on his coat of many colors to feign his death. Yet their wickedness had worked out for good: in a time of famine the brothers came to Egypt also, and Joseph, now in a position of power, apparently forgave them. There the Hebrew people as a people was born, born in immigrant quarters, born as the result of family strife—nevertheless, born. A new people existed, all of them descended from the patriarch Jacob, the old father of them all. Jacob moved to Egypt as well, and it seemed that all would be well for Israel. And then, Jacob, the patriarch, died and was buried back in the home cemetery. Now what?

After the funeral, many things are different. During the old father's lifetime, his son Joseph, powerful viceroy in Egypt, had treated his brothers and nieces and nephews well. It seemed he had forgiven them for kidnapping him and selling him into slavery. It *seemed* so. But what would happen now that their common father was gone? The floodgates of revenge will open now, people said. Not daring to face their powerful brother, the eleven sent a message saying, "Forgive, we pray you, the evil we did you. Forgive, for God's sake, forgive!" Joseph, hearing the message, wept. Notice the features of this story that are common to other human stories of loss and grief: There are human tears; there is often human resentment, too—resentment powerful enough to destroy even so strong a family as that of Joseph and his brothers.

In this life there do come opportunities for revenge, whether we are powerful Egyptian statesmen, or simply grieving family members. There has been a quarrel; there has been an injury to your integrity; your good faith has been doubted; your attempted kindness has been scorned. But now let us say that the tables are turned. You have a chance at last to get even. What will you do?

Joseph did two things, one negative and mistaken, one positive and Christlike. We had better look at both. First, his mistake. The brothers came back to see Joseph in the new circumstances. They prostrated themselves like subjects before an oriental monarch. "We are here as your slaves," they said. This was no metaphor. Joseph the ruler really had the power to sell them into slavery, just as once they had sold him into slavery. He had the power to harm them as once they had harmed him. What will his response be? Joseph answers, "I can't put myself in the place of God" [50:19 TEV]. Now this was Joseph's mistake. Certainly we see why he would have made it. Joseph here thought of God on the model of an oriental despot, reigning, ruling, disposing: God the Emperor, God the Pharaoh, God demanding that his followers cringe before him in fear. And Joseph thought, I must not be like that. I am only a family member; I am not a god.

But the long biblical story tells us that while God is indeed majestic, ruling and overruling in human affairs, that is not the whole truth. There is a deeper, more godlike note in God. That note is God's profound purpose to forgive. There is nothing deeper in God than mercy; there is nothing truer to the Bible story than God's forgiving love.

So when Joseph said, "I am not God," there was obviously a sense in which he was right, but a stronger sense in which he was very wrong. For he then did another thing, a thing that was utterly godlike. Joseph once again, in the new circumstances as before, forgave, fully and freely forgave, his evil brothers. "You did do wrong," he says, "but God turned your evil into good." My suffering at your hands was a part of God's providential purpose. "You have nothing to fear. I will take care of you and your children" [50:21 TEV].

Notice two things about this forgiveness. The first is that it is preceded by reproach. There can be no forgiveness if there is no sin. Some people think of forgiveness as if it meant being a perpetual ninny who never notices that anything is wrong. That's not forgiveness; it is moral idiocy. Of course there was something wrong. They had sold him into slavery. They had sinned. And if I know anything about being a brother, even during the Egyptian sojourn these brothers had sometimes cast a backward look, sometimes resented Joseph the viceroy, sometimes grumbled about his power over their lives. Let's get this straight, once and for all; Matthew, in the passage that the old baptists called the Rule of Christ, says, "If your brother does wrong, go and take the matter up with him, strictly between yourselves. If he listens, you have won your brother over." Note well, that calls for reproach—reproach leading to brotherly conversation. Often, such a reproach issues immediately in reconciliation. Not always, but often. So Matthew's Jesus goes on: "But if he will not listen, take one or two others with you, so that every case may be settled on the evidence of two or three witnesses. If he refuses to listen to them, report the matter to the congregation; and if he will not listen even to the congregation, then treat him as you would a pagan or tax-collector" (Matt. 18:15–18). In other words, treat him as someone whom Jesus loves, and starts out with from scratch, hoping for conversion, hoping to make that tax-collector, that outsider, a disciple. That is the Rule of Christ.

The happy case, then, is one in which forgiveness comes as soon as possible. And forgiveness is what Joseph then and there provided.

> "You meant to do me harm [That is Joseph's reproach, and as we have just seen, it is appropriate]; but God meant to bring good out of it by preserving the lives of many people, as we see today. Do not be afraid. I shall provide for you and your dependents." Thus he comforted them and set their minds at rest.
>
> [Gen. 50:20f.]

Maybe this explains why earlier Bible scholars said that Joseph is a "type" of Christ. We don't know what a *type* is, perhaps, and for all I can say today, we may never know. Yet part of its meaning is surely this, that in the Joseph story, we see Jesus' own story foreshadowed; we know that Jesus was one who came to forgive and to redeem; we know that the way he taught his disciples was a way of forgiveness; we know that he suffered much at the hands of others, not least at the hands of his own disciples; we know that after the resurrection, after Easter, the practice of forgiveness became central to the common life of the disciples. After Jesus had forgiven them, "he breathed on them, saying, 'Receive the Holy Spirit! If you forgive anyone's sins, they are forgiven'" [John 20:22–23].

So what about the injuries you and I have received or believe we have received? What shall we do now, to even up the score? "Ah," I can say, "I am not God. It is not my place to forgive all that wickedness." And the implication will be, "Maybe God will forgive them—but *I* don't mean to. Let them get what they deserve!"

On the other hand, there is this Joseph story. For here Joseph shows us beforehand what Jesus, too, will do when he has a chance to do it. The story replies to this excusing of oneself. It says, "No, you are not God—but you are God's deputies: God in Christ has breathed on you, has authorized you to forgive, and by forgiving, empowered you to set straight the score, once for all." For when we forgive, we share God's reconciling work on earth; when we forgive—Jesus says—we know ourselves truly forgiven.

Two weeks from now, our church is scheduled to commemorate Jesus' death and resurrection in the eucharist. If we celebrate this meal according to our regular practice, after the Scripture is read and the sermon preached, our offerings will be brought to the table, with the bread and wine of our meal, and we will say together a certain prayer. Let me read you that prayer, so that you can ask yourself now if you will be ready to pray it then:

> *Here, Lord, we return the fruit of our labor;*
> *here the bread we have earned by the sweat of our brow.*
> *Refresh us now with your presence,*
> *as we remember again, in these gifts,*
> *the gift without money and without price.*
> *If we have wronged anyone,*
> *we pledge to restore what can be restored;*
> *we here forgive any who have wronged us;*
> *and we humbly ask that with these gifts*
> *you receive us at this table, your repentant children, in the*
> *name of Jesus Christ our Lord. Amen.*

Enough Food for All

The first eucharist after the blowup in the church was bound to be a crucial time. It was important that matters be well managed. We met in our chapel, a smaller space than the regular meetingroom; it would be crowded if everyone came, but in it we would face one another as we worshiped. As the previous sermon had shown, one large issue before the church was forgiveness. Another, though, was the insecurity that gripped most of us when we asked how we would make it through the days ahead. What if alienated members simply ceased to attend? What if our thin lines of support gave way? What if the bills were not paid? What if the essential work of maintaining our common life were left undone? Were we not very likely to perish? Since the need for mutual forgiveness would certainly be addressed in the liturgy of the Lord's supper I decided that it was more fitting for the sermon to declare God's provision for our pressing needs. That, too, could be done in the spirit of the Lord's supper, since one of its leading themes is nourishment—in it God feeds us earthly food and heavenly food as well.

One of the strengths of our small fellowship, and of the denomination of which it was a part, was its traditional practice of meeting human need. It did this through churchwide programs that addressed hunger and homelessness at home and overseas as well. It also did it through participation in a local shelter program for the "street people" of our city. With other churches, ours took its regular turn in providing food and cooks and cleanup crews for a nightly free meal at the shelter. Many members of the congregation would not have dreamed of missing their turn working at the shelter. By analogy, then, God would not fail to provide for us—at least that is Jesus' argument according to Luke 11. I would proceed, however, not by such a direct argument from analogy, but by way of a narrative. As in the preceding sermon, the Old Testament provided the lively story I needed, in this case, the story of Israel fed with manna during its journey out of captivity.

Our Lord's supper rite called for a short sermon coming early in the service. Here it is.

If only we had died at the LORD's hand in Egypt, where we sat
by the fleshpots and had plenty of bread!   (Exod. 16:3)

[Also read John 21:9–17.]

If you are wandering in the desert with a crowd of people of all ages and sizes, you had better make sure of your supplies—especially supplies of food and drink. That was a lesson Israel was slow to learn. Back in Egypt almost everybody had a backyard garden; many had flocks and a few acres to graze them; there was always the open air market where one could buy grain, figs, dates, persimmons, even fresh meat—all a body wanted to live. But they had followed young Moses into the desert, and now look! Someone was always running out of something. There was plenty of grumbling: "Oh, for the leeks and garlic of Egypt." (Perhaps they hadn't been that fond of Egyptian leeks and garlic when there was no lack of it, but now, nothing sounded better.) Then came the real crunch. *They ran out of food.* The livestock was slaughtered and consumed, the pack animals, too. No flour and oil for bread. No dried dates and nuts. Nothing. Children were crying; parents were distraught; everyone murmured. Moses took the matter up with God, who simply said, "Wait until tomorrow morning." Needless to say, Moses was up by dawn, and many other Israelites with him. And sure enough, as soon as there was light enough to see, the ground was white as if frost or snow had fallen in the desert. "What is it?" people asked. (And that is why they called it *manna,* which in Hebrew means, "What is it?") What it was actually varied a good deal, depending on whom you talked with afterwards. Flakes or drops, round or flat, white or yellow— later, people remembered differently. At the time, though, it was above all wonderful, because it simply showed up on the ground to be collected. Manna (or "what-is-it") appeared again the next day, and the next, and the next, and the next. You could bake it; you could boil it; if you had cooking oil (which they did not), you could have fried it. What did it taste like? Again, memories differed; some said sweet, others, fatty, like nuts. In any case, it was good, and most of all, it was *food.* It came daily; everybody had enough and nobody had too much; it was like food from heaven. It *was* food from heaven.

When heaven provides, though, one has to be prepared for heaven's whimsies. On the first Friday of the manna a warning went out: "Today, gather manna as usual; it will keep for two days." Most did as they were told; they gathered enough for Friday and for the Sabbath to follow. A few, however, went out to gather on Saturday morning, and guess what: No manna on the ground! Israel's Lord had only obedient followers in mind when he provided enough food for all.

Now as I have told you, the stories about manna don't quite match; some tell the tale one way, some another. It doesn't really matter, though, because all this was a long time ago. Once the Israelites marched out of the desert into the Promised Land, the manna stopped. No one ever saw another morning like that wonderful first manna morning. It seemed only a story from the past. But was it only that?

For while the manna stopped, *God never stopped providing for God's people.* This is a historical fact. Israelites had trouble in the new land—trouble with idolatry (that was the worst); trouble with neighbor peoples (that was the bloodiest); trouble with one another (that was the nastiest). Yet in all the history recorded from their beginnings to the coming of Jesus (well over a thousand years) there is no record, inside the Bible or outside it, of famine or widespread food shortage that could destroy the people. Manna was no more, but God who provides was still God. And Israel kept on telling the story of the manna—we find it in Exodus, in Numbers, in Deuteronomy. We find it also in Psalm 78—one of the songs in the great hymnbook of the Jews. Listen to its verses:

Then he gave orders to the skies above
and threw open heaven's doors
He rained down manna for them to eat
and gave them the grain of heaven.
So everyone ate the bread of angels;
he sent them food in plenty

. . .

But still they wanted more.

{Psalm 78:23–30}

What is that last line about? Well, part of the story I have held back is that the Israelites were not satisfied with manna from heaven. Once they realized God would send it every day, they began to take manna for granted. Some didn't trust God to provide enough, and tried to gather twice their share. That didn't work. Once they stopped worrying about having enough to eat, they began to worry about its quality—manna didn't taste enough like leeks and garlic to suit their desert taste buds. That, though, is not today's story; we must save it for another time.

Even in the New Testament, Jews were still remembering the manna story. Do you recall the story of Jesus and the five thousand who were hungry? Jesus had them sit down (perhaps so no one would start pushing and grabbing?) and before long, everybody was fed—with bread and fish! When the leftovers were gathered, there were exactly twelve baskets full—which is to say, as many as the tribes of Israel? The God of the manna was the God of the twelve baskets? And when he was risen from the dead, Jesus met the disciples, and fed them bread and fish—hardly what you'd expect from a mere ghost. Once again, *there was food enough for all.*

Have you ever stopped to ask why the people of our denomination are busy every year, in most of our churches, furnishing food? Why is there a project to provide better farm animals overseas? Why is there a denominational volunteer service concerned with food for folk who don't live where we live? Why do members of this community care about *others* having enough to eat? Why are some of us cooking for the local shelter for the homeless? Why is it that not even a crafty beggar will be turned away hungry from one of our households? Oh, that's easy, you will say. Because it's right! Well, but how do we know it's right? Other people don't seem to know that. Other people in our society say, in effect, "Let 'em starve; it's not *my* family." So how do we know it's right? We know it is right because that is the way God treats us. God provides. Ever since the day of the manna, God has been providing. God *never* quits providing.

And now, you see, we get to the real point. God feeds the people because God is God. "Shall not the Judge of all the earth do right?" [Gen. 18:25 KJV]. Certainly God will do right. Then why are you so anxious about your life? Why are you so anxious about your church? Is it not God's life, granted to you? Is it not God's church, into which God has called you, rather than the other way around? And will God who sends the manna not continue to provide?

That is what this Lord's supper, this eucharist, is about: It says God feeds; it says God provides; it gives thanks that there is enough for all. When you come to this table, you signify, "I trust God. I trust Jesus. I trust the Spirit." To be sure, there is something left for you to do. The Israelites had to scoop up the manna. You and I have to scoop up the gifts God sets before us. But there wouldn't be much use scooping if God were not God. As for me, I intend to scoop.

SERMON 3

Starting Over

The invitations for me to supply Sunday sermons for our troubled congregation turned into a broader invitation to serve as interim pastor for an unstated period of time. It was generally understood that this interim could not be short in our case, since the congregation was in poor position to secure the sort of pastor we urgently needed to lead us out of our difficulties. Instead, we must recover from the worst of our troubles during an interim period, and I was to be hitched into the harness for that interim—if I stood up to the task. What sort of "first sermon," then, should I preach? Many a beginning sermon is programmatic, laying out the direction that a new leader proposes, perhaps in light of considerable thought and consultation. I felt this could not be such a sermon, for mine was an interim rather than an ongoing place. On the other hand, the church had made a positive move (as I saw it) in inviting me to serve, so that even in this case there was an element of beginning, of starting over, in the Sunday service whose bulletin would for the first time list me as "pastor."

This should be a time of getting acquainted in a new way. While I had gotten to know a few members of the congregation, to many, I was only a slender, graying figure who appeared along with other worshipers on Sundays—that and nothing more. It might be a good idea to let them see something of the human being beneath my Sunday suit. So there might well be a touch of autobiography in the sermon.

On the other hand, I was not the chief item faced by the church. The crisis that I have already described persisted. It was not clear how many members would continue to attend, how many would be discouraged beyond recall by the slow decline of our congregation that had issued in the recent disruptive events. The chief word we needed was a word of gospel cheer—the good news that comes through Jesus Christ. We had to learn to make gospel

sense of our present difficulties, and find our way forward in gospel terms. In these circum-
stances, I chose (or was led to) the text in Amos that appears here.

> The words of Amos, one of the sheep-farmers of Tekoa. He re-
> ceived these words in visions about Israel during the reigns of
> Uzziah king of Judah and Jereboam son of Jehoash king of Is-
> rael, two years before the earthquake. He said,
>
> > *The LORD roars from Zion*
> > *and thunders from Jerusalem;*
> > *the shepherds' pastures are dried up*
> > *and the choicest farmland is parched.*
> >
> > *Do two people travel together*
> > *unless they have so agreed?*
> > *Does a lion roar in the thicket*
> > *if he has no prey?*
> > *Does a young lion growl in his den*
> > *unless he has caught something?*
> > *Does a bird fall into a trap on the ground*
> > *if no bait is set for it?*
> > *Does a trap spring from the ground*
> > *and take nothing?*
> > *If a trumpet sounds in the city,*
> > *are not the people alarmed?*
> > *If disaster strikes a city,*
> > *is it not the work of the LORD?*
> > > *(Amos 1:1f.; 3:3–6)*

What is the word that Americans love most to hear? It is *success*. We
like to hear about athletes who soared to the top of their sport, about
companies that by their ceaseless energy drove their competitors to
the wall, about pop singers who were so successful no one can believe
they really died. To be an American is above all to win. Our favorite
story is about some lad or lass in some distant place—let us say a
Mongolian sheepherder—who all his youth dreamed of coming to
America, success-land, a lad who scraped and saved and finally did

come to America, started as a dollar-an-hour dishwasher, worked, scrimped, began a business importing Mongolian goat hair, monopolized the goat-hair industry, made billions of dollars, and now lives in retirement in Santa Monica, making everyone happy by giving back a few paltry millions of those he had acquired. That, we are told, is the American dream.

Notice how different, though, the favorite American story is from the favorite Bible story. The Bible rarely tells of anyone who got rich—an exception is that man who kept tearing down his barns so he could build bigger ones, only to discover at a crucial moment in his life that he had to die [Luke 12:16–21]. In the main, the Bible is not about getting rich. It is not even about succeeding. Ultimately, the Bible is about God, and God in the Bible seems most of the time to lose, not win. In Genesis, God created man and woman—you remember how that story turned into tragedy. In Exodus, God chose a people, Israel, to be faithful to him—God's missionary people to all the world. You remember how that story turned out, also. Finally, God sent a Son, a favorite, who would tell people about God so they would trust God not themselves. Jesus didn't let God down; he was faithful to the end. But you will remember that God seemed to lose that time, also. They crucified Jesus. God seemed always to be losing!

Is the Bible story, then, not about winning but about losing? Not quite that, either, for in the long run God's people do receive a blessing. God's way, however, is not a simple success story—from a Mongolian sheepfold to a mansion in Santa Monica, or from a log cabin to the White House—but is a story in which God deliberately leads human beings to try and try again. Adam and Eve, expelled from the Garden, had a chance to begin—human history. The people of Israel were often disappointing—but through them came the law and the prophets and the gospel. The cross of Christ was the worst deed in human history, but God turned that worst into the salvation of the world. Starting over from failed beginnings seems to be God's regular way.

Now we in our church have had some disappointment. We have

had some failure. There has been a setback. Never mind now about whose fault it is. What I want to show you is that whatever its cause, such a setback is a regular part of God's way with his people, for by the alchemy of grace, God who calls his people uses all that we have been, including our mishaps and our failures, to equip us for all that we shall become. *Starting over* is part, a central part, of the story of God.

You know that the prophets were God's chosen men and women. Yet how did the prophets become the messengers, the voices, that could point the way into the future? Quite simply, God again and again drove each prophet back to the beginning, requiring him or her to start all over once more.

A case in point is Amos. Who was Amos? Why, the Bible answers quite simply, he was "one of the sheep-farmers of Tekoa" [Amos 1:1], Tekoa being a small town southeast of Jerusalem. He was, in other words, a country lad, not used to city life, and not caring much for it, either. Moreover, Amos emigrated. At a time when Israel was divided, north and south, he left the familiar south country and went north to preach. Then he ended up being thrown out of town by a combination of religious and political authorities [Amos 7:10–13]. The better the prophet, the worse his fate!

But that is not the part of the Amos story I wish to show you today. Right at the beginning of his prophet ministry, Amos was required to start over. He was a sheepherder; he also ran a fig orchard. He was no preacher and no preacher's son, yet God said to him, "Go and prophesy to my people Israel." So Amos had to leave the ranch, leave the orchard, leave his home country, and go preach to those self-satisfied Northerners! Starting over.

Here is the truly interesting thing: When Amos began to preach, he found that the things he had learned as a rancher were extremely valuable in his new role. He saw that there is cause and effect in all God's world. Look, said Amos the preacher, "Do two walk together, unless they have made an appointment?" [3:3]. Look out there over the prairie. As far as you can see, nothing. There, from that direction, comes one Bedouin. From another direction, another

Bedouin. Suppose they meet, and then they continue in a certain direction together. Is their walking together to be considered a mere coincidence? Of course not. Is it then only a coincidence when God's people disobey, and disaster strikes? Amos the sheepherder had learned how life works; from that knowledge he saw how to begin as a prophet.

Brothers and sisters, my own life has not been an easy one. These hairs are not white, as you may suppose, from advanced age. These shoulders are not bent because of lounging about in some tropical resort. Time would fail to tell of the challenges I have faced: the bitter necessity to leave the seminary where I had begun teaching, the strange experience of becoming a kind of unofficial missionary, first in the Catholic University in San Francisco and then in other universities elsewhere, then in the Episcopal Seminary in Berkeley. I was treated with courtesy in those places, but always I remembered my baptism, my ordination, my brothers and sisters in the little churches like this one. And indeed, through all the twists and turns in my life I still worshiped and sometimes preached in churches such as this one, so there was a curious and often uncomfortable gap between my Sundays and my weekday labors. In all those places there were discouragements. I was dismissed by one university and unsought by others. I was misunderstood often, slandered at one university by a fellow professor, shunned by many. The marriage of my youth failed. My children apparently found the Christian journey too difficult for them and dropped out. Where was my long trail leading? Yet all the time, through all the backtracking, the disappointments, the fresh starts, God seems to have had a plan for my life, and the evidence for that is that God used all that I had been in order to remake my life when again and again I had to start over.

Starting over, though, is the story of God's church. Do you know about the life of John Wesley, the founding father of the Methodists and one of the great Christians of all time? Wesley got off to a bad start. The son of a clergyman, he went to Oxford—but not to have a good time! Rather with others he formed a "Holy Club," in which members would prove to themselves that they deserved to go to heaven. After college, Wesley accepted an appointment to become a missionary to Georgia in America—America being a notoriously hard place to minister! In Georgia he irritated the local Christians by forcing them to worship in ways they could not understand. Besides, Wesley fell in love with the eighteen-year-old daughter of the local bailiff. She, rather than take up with this serious clergyman, eloped with her boyfriend, whereupon Wesley excluded her from communion and got himself sued by her father in the local court. Not a good start, you will agree. The colonial records of Georgia include this entry:

> "Wesley, Jn. . . . . Brother of Charles; Minister at Savannah; embarked 14 Oct 1735; arrived Feb . . . 1736; run away [that is, run out of town] 3 Dec. 1737."

That is all. Is that the end of the story, though? Hardly! On the Atlantic crossing, Wesley met some Moravians, spiritual kin to baptists. They opened the Bible, explained it to him in a new way. When he got home at last, he visited the Moravian chapel at Aldersgate in London. There, one night,

> about a quarter before nine [he wrote], I felt my heart strangely warmed. I felt I did trust in Christ, Christ alone for salvation; and an assurance was given me that he had taken away my sins. . . .

John Wesley ministered for fifty years after that, became the leader in the greatest single evangelistic movement the world had ever known, the evangelical revivals, and was widely known for his wisdom, his patience, his fairness, and his faith. Yet all the teaching that Wesley later imparted to Methodists was already known to him when he was a member of the Holy Club in college, already known to him when he was a stuffy parson pursuing a Georgia maiden who had her mind on another man. God takes us as we are, with all the character and knowledge we have so far acquired, and uses those very qualities, transformed by the alchemy of grace, to equip us for all that we shall become.

Old Rudyard Kipling, the British author, was not far from the
Christian truth when he wrote the poem called "If."

> *If you can meet with Triumph and Disaster*
> *And treat those two impostors just the same;*
> *If you can bear to hear the truth you've spoken*
> *Twisted by knaves to make a trap for fools,*
> *Or watch the things you gave your life to, broken,*
> *And stoop and build 'em up with worn-out tools*

If you can live that way, Kipling concludes,

> *Yours is the Earth and everything that's in it.*

Jesus had said it first—Matthew 5:5: "the meek will inherit the
earth." Yet I wanted you to hear Kipling's version, also. We confront
losses; the tools with which we build now become worn out; but
with God's help we stoop and build again. It is what God did in
Jesus Christ. It is what God wants to do again in this church.

Starting over may be your own story, too. Christians have a name
for that kind of starting over; we call it "conversion." Conversion
and baptism don't mean just starting; they mean starting over. We
are not baptized at life's beginning; we are baptized after we realize
that by ourselves we make a mess of things, realize that there is no
way we can set them right, realize that for all that we ourselves have
done, God's will may be done in heaven but it is not being done on
earth, not where we live, anyway. When we can acknowledge that,
when we can admit in the words of the Proverbs that

> *A road may seem straightforward,*
> *yet end as the way to death {14:12},*

when we can say to God "not my will but yours be done," then God
is ready for us with a new start; God is ready to place our hands again
on the old tools; God is ready to transform our character into something of use in the kingdom of truth and love. That is true of our
church; that is true of our own lives. In fact, it is the gospel truth.

SERMON 4

Under Sealed Orders

For some New Testament scholars, the perplexing and difficult-to-interpret sayings of Jesus in the Gospels are like a puzzle to be solved or a scientific spot of ignorance to be erased: we must know all, understand all, rationalize all. For the preacher who serves as a pastor to Christ's flock, however, these difficult and mysterious sayings of Jesus seem remarkably similar to the perplexities and difficulties of gospel ministry. Often we must trust a Master whose way is not all plain, not all rationalized, not all evident. Certainly that was the case in our congregation, which had suffered severe setbacks, and for one reason or another could not see the road ahead. To such a congregation, the mysterious command given by Jesus to the seventy in the text for the following sermon might seem remarkably like their own circumstances. At least, that was the idea with which I began. The task of the narrative core of this sermon, then (drawing from Luke's description of the departure of the seventy on their mission task), was on the one hand to provide verisimilitude that would make the scene credible, and at the same time to recapture within it the bewilderment, the uncertainty, that made that primitive scene analogous to our own plight.

This sermon is a good illustration of what I have argued elsewhere (e.g. in my volume Doctrine, *44–46) is* the *baptist vision, which requires Christians to see things here and now in a shape or framework provided by particular parts of Scripture. This is, of course, a risky principle—it will be distorted, for example, by any who omit from it the centrality of Jesus Christ, so that they read in the Pentateuch a law that commands that a witch must be burned and conclude from it (a) that there must be witches here now, and (b) that it is a Christian duty to burn them. On the contrary, Jesus has come, and the dark powers of witchcraft are forever banished exactly by that coming; Jesus has come, and so even if any were thought to be a witch, violence is never-*

more the way of the people of God. So these distortions of the baptist vision can be avoided, as I hope they are here.

Another feature of this sermon that I note, reading back over it, is that it begins its use of analogy not with the central message I mean to convey (a message reflected in the sermon title) but by an appeal to a characteristic feature of our congregation—its fondness for remembering the old days. We looked backward with pleasure when some would have said that we needed most of all to look forward. I hoped to turn that fault (if it was a fault) into a virtue by using it to remind us of the inherent difficulty of being Christians together. Moreover, this starting point enabled me to begin where many listeners already were, in the hope of leading them from that place to where they needed to stand.

Who is to test, who is to see if the preacher has faithfully employed Scripture, faithfully read the present by way of the selected text, employing that vision only in light of the centrality of Christ Jesus? The answer is easy in the present case: it was the task of the congregation who heard the sermon to test its spirit (and every spirit) to see whether it came from God. So, in this sermon as in others, there was work for the listeners as well as for the preacher.

Carry no purse, no bag, no sandals, and greet no one on the road.

(Luke 10:4)

For young ministers starting out on the road to ministry, that is pretty poor advice, don't you think? Surely what you would want young ministers at the seminary to hear is just the opposite: "Get a bank account, and don't let the balance dip too low. Establish your credit; there will be a time when you'll need to make installment purchases. Wear nice shoes; people notice these things. Get some good luggage; you'll travel a lot. And whatever you do, be friendly to everyone." Isn't that the kind of advice Jesus should have been giving the seventy?

Well, perhaps things were different when Jesus briefed the seventy before they set out. How should we envision it? I imagine a scene of enormous tension. Not everyone is being chosen. Some do not have partners—so Jesus pairs them off with one another. The message is precisely repeated to these chosen couriers. The instructions are brief but explicit. Villages are designated, one, two, even three villages per pair of messengers. (Did Jesus check off the villages on a map he had made or copied?) With just this preparation they set out, not to be (as we so lazily say today) "witnesses in their daily lives"—of course, they were that—but under instruction to go to an exact place with an exact message in preparation for the mysterious future "coming" of the Lord. They traveled, we might say, *under sealed orders.* What it would all amount to would be known to no one until grave events had occurred yonder in the capital city. And then, then, after the great Passover, after the Easter rising, these villages of Galilee would be visited by the Lord himself, who would find the seeds of primitive Christianity already planted in each village by these forerunner disciple messengers. These Galilean hamlets were to be the hothouses of the unfolding Rule of God.

No doubt this was great business. There was excitement in the air and a sense of mystery. Do we catch the strangeness of those days? Did Jesus really tell them to "greet no one on the way"? And did they obey? Was a discipline of silence (perhaps for fear of spies) enforced upon the messengers as they traveled to their appointed villages? We are not unfamiliar with strange religious behavior. Some of us have seen Moonies or Haré Krishnas at the airport, most of us have seen Mormon missionaries making their starched way through a suburb, or Jehovah's Witnesses importuning at neighborhood doors. We should admit that some folk even find our own religious behavior strange! But this gospel scene is strange beyond all these comparisons. "Greet no one on the road." Silence. Tight-lipped, they set their faces to the appointed towns. Under sealed orders they march.

> *Whether beneath was flinty rock*
> *Or yielding grassy sod,*
> *They cared not, but with force unspent*
> *Unmoved by pain, they onward went*
> *Unstayed by pleasures, still they bent*
> *Their zealous course to God.*
>
> *{T. T. Lynch}*

In a way, this would explain this strange verse in Luke's Gospel. But what has all that to do with you and me here in this city in this present time? Answer: the first lesson of this text is that *being a disciple is hard.* Has anyone ever told you any of the stories about the old days in this congregation? I mean the old, old days, when the church was still downtown, and the beginnings were being made? About how much work there was to do, being a church in a town where most folk didn't go to church, a church where pastor and people worked together to make a go of it? And think what it meant when some came out to this new suburban site in the fifties—to what must then have seemed the very edge of things—to build a new building where few members lived, where there was no certainty of survival, where building the new congregation was just as hard as building the church building, or even harder. Do you ever sit around—I know you do—and talk about those old days and how hard they were?

Do you suppose the first-century Christians themselves sat around and talked over the very earliest days, remembering how hard they were? Then, if there was someone present who had "been with the Lord from the beginning," the old stories would come out. Is this what they would say?

"You youngsters think the work is hard today? Why, I remember when he sent out seventy of us, two by two, to carry a message he had trusted to us. No money allowed—and most of us had none, anyway: We had to depend strictly on the generosity of the people in the town where we were assigned. No weapons—he said we were lambs, not wolves. No baggage, even—we had to be free to move on a moment's notice from place to place. And no dallying with people we met on the way—it was all gospel business then, friend. We were to go into a village, find a place to sleep and eat, then heal the sick, preach the good news, move on. None of your settled congregations or your paid sermons—it was *rough* in the old days." Is that what they said?

Let an older member of this congregation give you younger

members some advice. When you hear people talking about the old days, and how hard it was then, if I were you, I'd believe them. I could tell you some stories like that from my own life. Things were hard in the last generation. Things are hard in *every* Christian generation. Oh, to be sure, the old-timers may exaggerate a bit, or forget a little, but my point holds. The Christian way is a severe way: it demands sacrifice of every disciple, and suffering, and discipline; certainly it makes those demands of any who go carrying the word.

So why should we not expect it to be hard in this generation? Why did we imagine that our foreparents, from Bible times right down to the generation just before us, would have it hard, but that suddenly, late in the twentieth century, everything would be soft and easy? Did we think we were God's all-time favorites? That there was no hard task for us? Baptism, the Scripture says, buries us with Jesus by baptism into *death!* (Romans 6:3). Whatever else that verse means, it surely means that the Christian way is a costly way, a sacrificial way, a hard way. If you had been looking for something else, you would not have followed a Savior whose emblem is a crucifixion. Had you been looking for something else, you would have not allowed the baptismal waters to close over your head. But if they did close over you, you belong to Jesus, and there is a price to pay.

Whenever a sermon is preached from this pulpit, it is appropriate for you to ask, Where is the *good* news in this sermon? When there is no good news, the gospel has not yet been preached. So where is the good news in this strenuous text: "Carry no purse, no bag, no sandals, and greet no one on the road"?

To answer, let me remind you of the secrecy with which Jesus sent out the seventy. Perhaps he whispered his instructions to them. Certainly he told them, "greet no one on the road"—for who knows whether spies from the Sadducees, or King Herod, or the Roman occupation force might be on the road also. More important still, the seventy could not know what their orders meant. They could not know, because Jesus had not told them what would happen *after* he went to Jerusalem. They could not know, because they were too deaf and blind to take in what was going to happen *in* Jerusalem. So they went with their message to the villages, unaware of all that the mission would mean. They journeyed, as it were, *under sealed orders. And is that not like our church as well?*

Sometimes, under the exigencies of business competition or the demands of wartime secrecy, the captain of a ship will be given sealed orders. They are enclosed in an envelope with a wax or metal seal, and the seal is not to be broken until the ship has cleared the harbor, the pilot has gone ashore, and the vessel is on the high seas. Then and only then the ship's officers are allowed to break the seal and discover their destination.

I think our church, these days, is like that ship. We know very well that we have a journey to take, and we know that it is not going to be easy. We are not going to quit; we have signed up for the duration; our loyalty is not to be questioned. But now we have left the familiar dockside. The lines fastening us to the old shore, lines long in place and green with moss, have been cast off. We have moved through the waters of the harbor that we know so well; we have left the familiar shore sightings astern. Out ahead, over the open ocean, there is a bank of fog, and we do not know what lies beyond that fog. Our orders are on board, but it is too soon for us to open them and learn our destination.

I have heard varied suggestions concerning our church's destination. Some think that our church will die. Perhaps it will indeed sink like a ship settling into the briny deep—but, brothers and sisters, if this is Christ's church, let us quietly agree that we will die first.

Some think that our church will now attract a young, vibrant pastor who will bring in families with small children. Perhaps this is so, but we do not yet know it. There is some fog ahead.

Perhaps our mission will be to bring in many our own age—the lonely, the ill, the heartbroken, the sin-sick—who will come to us as hungry birds fly to a feeding station when they discover that here there is friendship, here there is healing power, here there is heartbalm, here there is forgiveness and a chance even now to start over again. Perhaps. We do not know. There is the fog ahead.

What we do know is this: the Christ who has cut our orders is here with us in the ship, standing on the bridge. It is not what we shall be that matters most—it is the sealed orders from our ship's Captain.

I ask you to have faith. But not faith in me—that is arrogance.

I ask you to have faith. But not faith in the church—that is idolatry.

I ask you to have faith in Christ, who sends us out *under sealed orders,* saying,

> Go on your way. See, I am sending you out like lambs into the midst of wolves. Carry no purse, no bag, no sandals, and greet no one on the road.   [Luke 10:3–4]

With Basin and Towel

Many Christians regard the command of Jesus in John's Gospel ("wash one another's feet"—John 13:14c) not only as symbolic guidance for their attitude toward fellow believers, but also as instruction for a regular act of Christian worship: not only are Christians to baptize and preach and break bread together; they are also literally to wash one another's feet. The Roman Catholic church fulfills this command at least in the person of the pope, who each year at the paschal season ceremonially washes the feet of a poor man brought in from the streets of Rome. Many other Christians, however, regard this ceremonial action as enjoined not only for high leaders but for each believer. So it was in the congregation I served. Twice a year, at an appointed time before Easter and before Thanksgiving, the church gathered in the evening, not for the usual Lord's supper alone, but for a Love Feast that incorporated a simple meal, preceded by a ritual washing of one another's feet. The congregation gathered first in the usual meetingroom for a brief devotional with song and prayer. Then all retired to prepared rooms, one room for men and another for women, where basins of warm water stood ready. All were seated in a row, and then one member put on a long, white apron, placed the basin before his or her neighbor, and washed the neighbor's feet and dried them with the apron. Then both stood and embraced or kissed, and the neighbor with washed feet took a turn with the apron to wash the feet of the next in line, and thus, until the last had washed the feet of the first. The brothers and sisters then met in the social hall where a hearty soup and bread were served. At the climax, one participant led the prayers that are enjoined in the words of institution ("For I received of the Lord that which also I delivered unto you, that the Lord Jesus, in the night in which he was betrayed, took bread, and when he had given thanks, broke it . . ."), and so the fellowship, reciting those words together from memory, broke the hard breads

that lay on the table, followed by the cup, and ended the night with a song of praise to the Crucified.

The sermon printed here, however, was preached at the more frequent Sunday morning Lord's supper. Our Sunday morning practice sets the context of the sermon: Before the regular liturgy of the table, we provided a children's agape, that is, a little symbolic meal, for (un-baptized) children only, to give them a share in the morning's events. The claim of the sermon is that as children have but a dim understanding of what their agape meal is about, so we baptized believers have but a dim understanding of the way of the cross. Yet we take that way, guided by these way-signs of bread and wine and the washing of feet that God has provided.

It was before the Passover festival, and Jesus knew that his hour had come and that he must leave this world and go to the Father. He had always loved his own who were in the world, and he loved them to the end.

The devil had already put it into the mind of Judas son of Simon Iscariot to betray him. During supper, Jesus, well aware that the Father had entrusted everything to him, and that he had come from God and was going back to God, rose from the supper table, took off his outer garment and, taking a towel, tied it round him. Then he poured water into a basin, and began to wash his disciples' feet and to wipe them with the towel. . . .

After washing their feet he put on his garment and sat down again. "Do you understand what I have done for you?" he asked. "You call me Teacher and Lord, and rightly so, for that is what I am.

"Then if I, your Lord and Teacher, have washed your feet, you also ought to wash one another's feet."

(John 13:1–5, 12–14)

On a recent Sunday I was asked to preach at another church. Before the service I read the printed bulletin. Among many other items there, hymns, announcements, sermon, and the like, I found toward the beginning a single line, marked "Communion." What did it mean, standing there by itself, I asked an early comer to the service. He answered, I thought, as if he were talking to a stranger off the streets. "Oh, that's when we have a little bread, drink a little juice." Startled by this description, I gathered that the church planned at that place in the service to commemorate the death and resurrection of Jesus Christ in his broken body and shed blood. The single bulletin line, "Communion," signaled the holy action: "This do in remembrance of me." But what a strange way, I thought, to talk about it—"have a little bread, drink a little juice." It sounded more like snack time in kindergarten. Did my fellow Christian speak to me that way because he thought me dim-witted? Or was it really the member himself to whom this saving sign was nothing more than "a little bread, a little juice"? I did not know.

Certainly I would hope that each one here today knows why we are gathered, knows what the elements of bread broken and wine poured represent, knows what God does in our midst in this thanksgiving meal. On eucharist Sundays we make this action central just because of what it means: We know who died and rose again; we know how we stand as Jesus' followers; we know what we pledge to God and one another when we eat at this table.

And yet there is a sense, a deeper sense, in which we do not know what these things mean, do not know what we do here. Jesus said it to Peter at the washing of feet:

> You do not understand now what I am doing, but one day
> you will.   (John 13:7)

There is a dimness in Peter's understanding, a veil that keeps him from catching on. To break through that veil, to show what his whole ministry is about, Jesus has taken a path that will lead to a cross. But he already knows they will not comprehend that, and so on the evening that we recall as Good Friday he eats with them a farewell meal that signifies beforehand the great sign of the cross and the resurrection. Yet Jesus reckons (or is it John the evangelist, recalling all this, who reckons?) that the followers will not get that, either; therefore, before the supper Jesus in this Gospel takes basin and towel and washes the others' feet. One day, he says, they will remember this and comprehend, even though they do not do so now.

How much understanding, then, is enough? Well, perhaps it depends upon where we are in faith's journey. The children here (and some of the rest of us as well) are in a time of preparation. This is why we have the children's love feast, the children's agape (a word which means love). Is it to them only a pleasant time with cookies in church? Perhaps. But we think a later time will come when the childlike rite of sharing the cookies will work its way into their full awareness that God is love [1 John 4:8].

How much understanding, then, is enough for us? Think of Jesus with the disciples in those tense last days. He had started a revolutionary movement. What kind of revolution was it? Palestine was an occupied country. Some said the future for Israel lay in cutting a deal with the Romans. That was the view of the high priests' party, King Herod's party. Some said the way to counter Rome was to move to the Dead Sea, start there a sect in hiding. Those were the Essenes. Some said there should be armed revolt—these were called Zealots. Where did Jesus stand? With none of the above, we would say today, but that was not so clear to the disciples. They were waiting, unsure which of these options he would choose, waiting for him to make his move. Some had gotten hold of swords, just in case Jesus expected Zealot violence of them. The point is that they didn't know for sure, and all his attempts to explain had failed.

Meanwhile, there was mistrust within the ranks of the movement. Apparently there was a spy or traitor among the innermost twelve. But who was it? If Jesus knew, he hadn't said.

Facing these difficulties without and difficulties within his movement, what should Jesus have done? For a modern revolutionary, maybe the answer would be, "Purge! Put on a trial. Accuse the guilty ones, and throw them out." Jesus had a different answer, as we read in John 13:3–5:

Jesus, well aware that the Father had entrusted everything to
him . . . rose from the supper table, took off his outer garment
and, taking a towel, tied it round him. Then he poured water
into a basin, and began to wash his disciples' feet and to wipe
them with the towel.

If you want to know what the new Rule of God is like, he was
saying, just look here. This is the sign of God's realm; this is what
this supper is about: not a purge, but love and forgiveness, humble
service to one another, helping one another come clean. Against the
Roman legion—the basin of water; against the Zealot guerrilla
army—the towel; against all earth's proud power—the sacrificial
way of love.

We smile sadly, perhaps, at a congregant who can sum up the
Lord's supper as "eat a little bread, drink a little juice." Joyfully we
smile at little children who understand little. Yet do we know what
we do when we break this bread and drink this cup? Does anyone
fully know? Perhaps we only know when we follow Jesus all the way
into the land of unlikeness [W. H. Auden], only know when we find
the cross and take it up as the shape of our own lives. Perhaps only
then do we understand the ministry of Jesus that becomes by his gift
our ministry as well. Meantime, the sign we do not fully understand
is still a sign for us. We have the basin and towel to help us understand this holy feast. We have the feast, this supper of memory and
hope, to help us understand the cross of Christ. And we have that
cross to help us understand the God we serve. We smile at the little
children. Does God perhaps smile at us?

PART TWO

The Recovery of Hope

(Twelve Sermons)

Finding a Life Worth Living

There comes a time in the life of a Christian community recovering from serious trouble when it must cease to concentrate upon that trouble alone and must move forward. While the earliest sermons I preached in one church in trouble attempted to make gospel sense of its troubles and thus transfigure them, we could not be forever focused upon reproach and forgiveness alone; there had to be a positive gospel message if we were indeed to be the church. My idea, and one that found support from congregational leaders as we talked it over together, was a workshop, *a day-long session that would help change our focus from grief and forgiveness (on which we had individually and collectively spent a good many weeks) to the recovery of hope and direction.*

Such a workshop could not achieve its goal if there were no preparation for it, and one bully pulpit for readying the congregation was—the pulpit. I preached three short series of sermons—a series on membership, one on ministry, one on mission—all aimed at defining afresh the very thing that we would seek collectively to grasp in the workshop, namely, our reason for being the church, our destiny as a part of God's people.

Yet this move forward must not carelessly ignore the actual dissension and despair that remained with us. We were not dead, but we were in mortal danger. I thought it best, then, to begin the sermon that would introduce the plan for a workshop with a reminder of death—one drawn from an event recently in the news as I prepared and preached the sermon. My main vehicle, though, would be a New Testament story, the familiar one of Philemon, Onesimus, and the apostle Paul. Its themes, for my purposes, were nicely summarized in a verse from another of Paul's epistles, 1 Corinthians 14:1: "Pursue love and strive for the spiritual gifts, and especially that you may prophesy." That verse, with its terms of art (unique biblical expressions such as "spiritual gifts," "prophesy") was not likely to mean much concretely to our folk. Yet if the Philemon story could provide substance, the two passages together—the single verse from First Corinthians and the whole short epistle or letter called Philemon— might yield a sermon. Let us see.

> Pursue love and strive for the spiritual gifts, and especially that you may prophesy.   (1 Cor. 14:1)
>
> [Also read Philemon.]

Last week Washington insiders were stunned to learn of the death of a highly placed official, deputy counsel to the president of the United States, apparently by suicide. Why would a forty-eight-year-old lawyer, the very epitome of success, destroy his own life? The answer was not clear. The papers said this was a man devoted to his family and his work, but with outside interests as well—theater, museums. No one suspected any trouble save the trouble hard work causes everyone. And of course, "apparent suicide" means that much is left untold—who knows the whole truth here? Nevertheless, such sad things happen. While you and I know people lying in hospital beds who struggle to recover and live, while we know people out of work who are tireless in seeking a decent job and the very means of life, there are others who have all these things, yet despair of life and destroy themselves.

This is not a sermon about suicide; that must come another day. It is about life, and concretely, about a life worth living. Today we are nearer the center of our faith; now we ask, how does one find a life worth living? The answer I propose is clear: *Only ministry makes life worth living.* That is Jesus' answer, as given in Mark 10:45: He said "the Son of man" (or as I prefer to translate it, "the Truly Human One") "comes not to be ministered to but to minister, and to *give* his life"—not by suicide, but in debonair self-surrender. Yet someone will say, That was perhaps all right for Jesus, but I want to know about my life now.

Let me respond by telling a story. This is the familiar story behind Paul's letter to Philemon. Modernizing the names a bit, there was once a man named Phil, a prominent leader in the church in

Colossae. Phil was not a clergyman (they didn't *have* clergy, as I understand New Testament history), but he was a leader in the church. Probably without him there would have been no church in his city. He recruited others to be Christians; he made his home available for church meetings; he seemed a model Christian. In Phil's household lived a youth named Sim. Perhaps Paul the Missionary had been a guest in that wealthy household, and perhaps Sim had waited on him as a servant. In any case, Paul knew Phil the rich Christian; Paul also knew Sim the servant. Sim had not become a Christian—he was restless and undecided; he didn't know what to make of his considerable skills, didn't know what to make of his life. Now came the trigger event: Some time after Paul's visit and departure, Sim ran away.

Bible students will remember something I have not mentioned: Sim (whose full name was Onesimus) was a slave. Yet that can be misleading. Slavery for first-century Greeks was not the harsh, racist institution we conceive. A slave might be more like an adopted child—he might expect to be set free when he was mature, and he might even become a proper family member. So Sim's running away may have grieved Phil the Christian more than it deprived him. We do not know what the relations were between these two men. Why had Sim not become a Christian? We do not know that, either.

What we do know is that when Sim ran, he ended up running to Paul. Since he was a traveling missionary, Paul was by this time in another city, perhaps Ephesus, and he was in jail for doing the things that missionaries usually do. Sim found him there, waited on him as a young man can wait on an older one, and before long, Paul led Sim to Christ.

When you become a Christian, things have got to change. For Sim, the big issue was the unfinished business back in Colossae, his rupture with Phil the master. If he went home to Phil, Sim could legally be fined, flogged with a whip, even crucified! Even if none of that happened, there was the broken human relation with Phil to be mended. And if Sim took the longer look, there was the question, what would become of his life if he went back to the place where he had been so restless, so unhappy, that he had run away. Staying with Paul now, he was a kind of assistant missionary. What would he become, this talented youth with a criminal past, if he returned to the old home in Colossae? Should he remain a fugitive, or go back and face the music?

We can deduce Sim's own answer from the letter Paul wrote to Phil—to Philemon, that is. Paul wrote on Sim's behalf, asking Phil to take Sim (or Onesimus) back, not as a slave, but rather as a brother, "very dear to me, and still dearer to you, both as a man and as a Christian" (Philem. 16).

How did it all come out? We don't know—which gives me, as storyteller, a good deal of latitude, you must admit! But consider the probabilities. If Sim had not been a changed youth, he would never have accepted Paul's offer and the letter we know would never have been written. If Phil had received this letter but angrily crumpled it and thrown it away, we would likely never have heard the story I am telling you. The probability, then, is that Paul's letter worked: Sim got, not the punishment he may have feared, but a new status in the household; Phil got, not the justice he may have preferred, but a new younger brother; and the people of God, thanks to the gifted Paul the reconciler, got a story that Christians have treasured for near two thousand years. Sim the upstart, the rebel, the restless, became Sim the younger brother, almost as in Jesus' parable of the prodigal son [Luke 15]. Sim found a life worth living. And Phil the loyal Christian leader, the reliable, the one who would never run away, found his household surprisingly changed. Can you believe that Phil found his own life starting over, as well?

Remember that this sermon is for us. My claim here is that life is worth living only if it is ministry, only if it is service under the banner of the great servant Jesus Christ. We have been learning, these weeks, that ministry does not begin when the church finds a new pastor; ministry does not happen when the clergy take charge. Ministry is complete, whole, entire only when Christ is present in fullness so that Christ ministers through each and all together. What we want to know is, how can this happen? If we are not paid church employees—and at this point *no one* in this church is—if we each have to earn our own living, care for our own households, then how can we truly be ministers? How can we in Jesus' words live our lives "not to be ministered to, but to minister, and to give our lives" [Mark 10:45]?

Let me show you three elements in the story of Phil and Sim that provide an answer to this question. All three are conveniently found in another sentence from Paul's writings—see 1 Corinthians 14:1.

The obvious key to the Phil and Sim story is *love.* There is the love of Jesus that converted Paul, and later transformed Phil the leader, and still later made Sim the servant a new man. Without Christ's love, none of these things would have happened. Yet Christ is not the only lover here. Don't you suspect that there was love between Phil and Sim, even before the story I am telling you began? This is a guess, but it is not a wild guess. This deserted master and his deserting servant cared about each other. Their love may have been unskillful and even angry or resentful, but love it was. Love comes in many forms, and one is the love between master and servant or father and son. Certainly, too, there was the genuine human love of Paul the Missionary, who loved them both and sought to bring them back together. And finally, if the story has the happy ending we reckon it has, there is the joyous love of the younger brother come home to be a brother, and the older brother converted anew to love a servant transformed into a Christian and friend. Here is the prodigal son story come true in real life, and (as it should) come true with an ending made happy by love.

So love is the theme, and many have experienced and explored it, from Jesus Christ to Sigmund Freud, from the great novelists to the simplest child. Love is what makes the human world go 'round. Yet without something else, love is not enough. Love alone often fails.

Besides love, then, what does it take to make a life worth living? Our text suggests that loving takes some skills, and in Scripture, these skills are called *gifts.* Again and again the apostle Paul writes about them. Some are gifted in leadership, some in counseling, some in healing. In worship, some sing great music, some arrange beautiful flowers, some preach. Not every skill in the Christian life is a distinctive gift—all members are witnesses, all without exception; all pray, without exception; all give, without exception. Yet beyond these elements of Christian life, there are special gifts that do distinguish us one from another. What was Sim's special gift? We are not told, though Paul's letter makes it clear that he has one: Sim is "now useful indeed" (Philem. 11).

Much of our life together in church involves discovering the special gift of each. Some of you have discovered a special gift God has given you, and you have been using it for Jesus' sake. Perhaps it is time for you to find yet another? Others are still waiting to discover their gifts, and indeed, some are waiting to take the first step of pledging their lives to Jesus as they accept his gift of life. But God has a gift for each. God will not let your gift be neglected any longer than you neglect to ask for it and receive it. God has a great plan for your life, no matter what you are now. If you think this is not your case, remember: That is what Sim thought, too, when he ran away! It was only when he sought out Paul, and yielded his life to Jesus, that Sim discovered that life could be worth living.

So how do we find our way to our own gifts? That requires the third thing, and this third thing was the special gift of the prophetic Paul. The Bible calls it *prophecy.* Perhaps today we would call it *gospel insight.* In any case, it was what helped Paul, first to guide Sim to Christ, and then by way of the letter to help Phil apply his gift so that Sim and Phil could get things straight between them.

Here we see that there is a special role in Christian ministry, not only for all the others, but also for the preacher, the prophet, as well. For the preacher of the gospel must be one who, like Paul the preacher, has the gift of prophecy, the gift of insight, that enables him or her to see what God is trying to do, and to help us each contribute to that doing.

Love, gifts, prophecy: the ambience of love, without which I am nothing [1 Cor. 13:2]; the unique flowering of a gift in each, so that together we may find lives worth living; the pervasive gospel guidance that is here called prophecy, by which we can know *how* to love, know *what* our gift is, and thus find a way to merge it with the gifts of others. Love, gifts, prophecy, or if you like, love, gifts, and the gospel that molds these two together. These are the secret keys that unlock the cage of constraint that confines us. Here are the three pass keys to a life worth living, the secrets of Christian life itself.

Now we come back to the beginning—to suicide, to despair, to the rejection of God's good gift of life. Clearly suicide is contrary to the good news that God gives us a life worth living all the way. But that applies to the church as well. Some in this place have spoken with despair of our fellowship, and I recognize that there is some cause for despair. Yet I am persuaded that God intends for us life, not death.

For that reason, I am now asking this church to gather in a workshop to study and to discover afresh this church's ministry, its own special gifts. We would gather on a Saturday, probably in late September, after proper preparation. We will not focus, in the workshop, upon the pastor-to-be whom we shall soon seek, but upon the church's ministry-to-be, upon its membership, upon its mission. We would seek to release our love, seek to identify our gifts, seek to place each gift and all our love within a prophetic frame of purpose. Only in that context can we know what kind of pastor we are to call. We would focus on the ministry of each, on the ministry of all. We will do this, I believe, because in words suggested by the Psalm [118:17], "We shall not die, we shall live, and do the work of the Lord."

So what about suicide? Suicide is a terrible threat to some. They feel an almost irresistible urge to destroy that part of God's good creation that is themselves. Let me say, as your pastor and your friend, if ever you confront such an urge, do not take it as God's word to you. God's word does not come that way, and that is not what it says. If you confront such an urge, call upon your church, call upon your pastor, call upon your Christian friends to pray with you. We read terrible suicide stories, and hear them often. Do we know the far more frequent but less told stories of those who feel that dread destructive urge, but resist it, overcome it, and thereafter live rich and useful Christian lives? "We shall not die, we shall live!" And that, I believe, is God's message to this church. Let us not destroy this fellowship, God's gift to us. Let us live, together live, and do the work of the Lord.

Contagious Christians

Perhaps the biggest visible need our church faced was growth. Whatever its theory of evangelism may have been, in reality the congregation depended upon biological growth—young families would have babies who would grow up in the church and be added to its number—and growth by transfer—since many Americans wanted to move to Southern California to make a new home. Neither of these means was providing actual growth: our families had grown older, and their children had matured and moved away; there was no longer a steady stream into our region of immigrants from eastern states. We were thrown back upon the elemental need of the Christian church at all times: evangelize or die.

Yet evangelism did not come easily to us. How distressing it would be, some of us felt, to talk to an outsider about religion—a subject so intimate we could barely discuss it with those nearest to us! Isn't it impolite to talk with others about their faith? After all, don't they have a right to privacy? And isn't religion a private matter? Religion in our culture seems to occupy the privileged role of the undiscussible that had once been occupied by the no longer sacred topic of sex. One does not discuss religion, and one refers to it only indirectly. That these cultural assumptions have antigospel implications seemed not to occur to most members.

Here, then, was an area where a change of the church's common mind was simply essential to achieving the new life we had to realize. The question was how to bring the change about, how to make what seemed the most natural of attitudes in the New Testament a conceivable, even a likely attitude for our folk. My idea in this sermon was to appeal to the contagious nature of holiness and unholiness—a primitive idea, but one (as Mary Douglas in Purity and Danger *has shown) that is still powerfully present in today's culture. Thus I invoke here one cultural phenomenon (contagion in the anthropological sense) and its biblical*

outworking in order to combat another cultural phenomenon (the excessive privacy that iso-
lates even Christians from others).

> The LORD told Moses to say to the whole Israelite com-
> munity: You must be holy, because, I, the LORD your God,
> am holy.   (Lev. 19:1–2)

> Brothers and sisters, join in imitating me.   (Phil. 3:17a NRSV)

There is a fragile but growing sense of evangelism here. Its signs
are everywhere visible. Many of you have attended the summer
Wednesday evening meetings focused on growth. At the corner outside our building, a new banner flutters in the breeze, telling even
speeding motorists that we are alive and meeting here. Every week,
some church members bring their friends, and their friends' friends,
to services. We hesitate on the edge of new growth like a rosebud
waiting to open in the sunlight. Yet something of utmost importance must happen before the bud opens: We ourselves must be clear
what it means to invite others to join us. What *is* membership?
Membership in God's great kingdom, membership in God's people,
but in particular membership in this fellowship, this particular
body of Christ meeting at this corner location week by week? This
prelude to evangelism is not to be skipped; with your support, I propose to devote these four remaining summer sermons to it, and first
of all, this one today.

It is no accident that we meet once more at the Lord's table on its
appointed Sunday. For the eucharist is the great biblical sign of ongoing membership in Christ and church, just as baptism is the great
biblical sign of starting out as a member.

Today I want to show you that being a member, being a real
Christian, is in one way like being a member of a club, or a member
of a business, or a member of a team. In all such cases, there is both
invitation and acceptance. You are drafted onto the team; you are
invited to be a partner in the firm; you are tapped for the club. If you
agree to join, that clinches it. You are in. But in another way being a

member of Christ and church is like being a member of a family, or belonging to a race of people. In such cases you have no choice; it simply happens that you are born a Smith or a Schwarz, that you are born an Asian or a Black or a White or something in between. This is a status that we acquire without accepting it and that we cannot effectively refuse. For us, the puzzle is this: How can being a member of Christ's community be both—how can it be both something we are given (a matter of grace) and something we grasp (a kind of human action)? Both gift and gumption? Both our destiny and our deed? The answer, I say, lies in the contagious nature of Christian existence, and contagion is our topic today.

In the more remote forms of human society, there was a division of all that is into the holy, the unclean, and the in-between. The gods were holy, and what they touched was holy; things crooked or corrupt or rotten were unclean; anything else was in between. But there was a complicating factor in this primitive system: If you were in between, and you touched the unclean, it made you unclean. *And if you touched or were touched by the holy, you became holy, too.* Of course, that is far too simple an account of our primitive ancestors' thinking, but it will do for now. For the enduring power of that thinking is evident today.

Suppose we had here on the table an animal, say a rat or a snake, that had died of natural causes. Would you freely put your hands on it, pick it up, handle it? Many of us would if we needed to, even with our bare hands. And yet, "with bare hands" indirectly expresses a certain reluctance, does it not? Why would we hesitate? Of course, because we don't want germs. Yes, but these feelings of reluctance were not born with the germ theory, which was only put forward in the last century. Even our most remote ancestors, who knew nothing of germs, felt this reluctance: It was their sense of the contagion of the unclean. If we touched it, our hands would be unclean, we would be unclean, and we would want to wash our hands, even if some biologist assured us there were no germs present. Uncleanness is *contagious,* and by touching we catch it.

Yet the other side holds, too. Our ancestors felt that if you were in-between and came into close contact with the truly holy, you would become holy, also. People felt this in Jesus' day; they reached out to touch his garments and draw on his holiness [see Matt. 14:35f.]. And if we do not readily sense these feelings, perhaps this is because something else has come to change our thinking. That something is the advanced awareness that the holiness of God is not just ritual purity; holiness is a matter of what you do, a matter of what you are. Already the Old Testament teaches this advanced theme—see Leviticus 19:2:

> You must be holy, because I, the LORD your God, am holy.

And immediately next, Leviticus repeats some of the Ten Commandments: Honor parents, keep the Sabbath, make no idols; God is God. The point is this: People who come close to God will act as God acts; their lives will by contagion be holy lives. On this view holiness is still catching, but now what one catches is not just a status, but a way of life to be lived.

Remembering that holiness works in this way helps us make sense of Paul's word to the church at Philippi. These church members had strong disagreements, which Paul put down to selfishness and jealousy [see Phil. 2:3]. The cure, he told them, was to follow his own example. "Be like me," Paul says in Philippians 3:17. Now that might strike cynical folk today as the height of folly. Did Paul think he was perfect? Certainly not! Then when he invited the others to copy him, wasn't he taking a foolish chance? For what if they copied his admitted faults, and justified themselves by saying, See, Paul did it, so it must be all right. Such thinking has led some to say, "Do as I say, not as I do." Yet Paul on the contrary had the courage to say, "Copy me!" Why? Is it not this? Paul had been near the risen Christ, on the road to Damascus and often since. From Christ he had caught the contagion of Christian living. And so in his letter he says to the others, "Come near Christ, and (in the ways that matter) you will of course be like me."

If Paul were here today, he would be a great worry to some present-day Christians. They suppose that such an *imitative* understanding of salvation and church membership misses the point, the inner mystery, the holy grace of salvation. They would want to say more about inward faith and less about being like Christ. But don't you see that nothing *could* be more mysterious—or more inward—than the contagion by which those who come near Christ catch the contagion of his faith, catch the passion of his love, catch the power of his hope? In fact, this is the old original biblical salvation mystery, the mystery of a God who says, "Be holy, for I am holy."

Furthermore, this way of thinking is deeply located in the baptist or Radical Reformation or Free Church way of understanding Christian existence. Why do God's people in this tradition spend so much time thinking about mission? Why do they work so hard to see that the hungry are fed and the homeless are housed and the sick are healed and the ill-clothed are covered? Is it not this? These folk believe Jesus cares about these things. Jesus is not busy making war—that is the business of the prince of darkness. Jesus is not busy cheating and stealing and gouging and lying to get ahead—that is the business of the world that does not know Jesus. Jesus came to heal the sick; Jesus came to forgive sinners; Jesus came to reconcile enemies; Jesus came to make peace. If we draw near to him, we are bound to imitate him and make these very things our own concern. Such internalized contagious nearness is not just the result of salvation, not just the added duty of some Christians with special callings, not just the occasional fruit of Christianity mainly busy about other matters. Nearness to Jesus in everything *is* Christianity; it *is* salvation; it is salvation come to your house, and yours, and yours [cf. Luke 19:1–9].

Sometimes when people talk about the Lord's supper, they wonder how sanitary it is to drink from a common cup or how appropriate it is to eat bread that other hands have handled. I will tell you that one of the last things I do before coming to preside at the Lord's table is to wash my hands, just as I would do if I were preparing food for guests in my own kitchen. I don't think we have much to fear in that regard here. Yet there is another kind of contagion at this table that you need to know about. If you are going to "commune" with people in this church, if you are going to hang out with these truth-tellers, these family-lovers, these sharers of all earthly goods, these followers of Jesus—if you stick around with the people who eat this holy meal, you are in actual danger of catching a life like Jesus' life. You risk becoming a Christian, here. So beware! Christianity is a holy contagion. Christians are contagious!

There is a related danger at the table itself. Suppose you are one of those Christians who has been holding something or other back from Jesus. I don't know what it is, but you know. Maybe you are withholding a little bit of loyalty, as if to say, "I'll wait and see how things work out at this church. If all goes well, fine. If not, I'll drop out." Maybe that was what some of the disciples at the Last Supper were thinking, too. Some of them even tried dropping out for a time after he was crucified. What they had overlooked, though, was the contagion of Jesus himself. They had eaten with him, eaten his food and drunk his drink. They had caught the contagion. Afterwards, none of them were happy again until they followed him all the way. So Christianity is both a gift and an achievement, both faith and work, to use the old terms. It's something you catch—or rather, something that catches you. Yet what is caught is a way of life, a pattern of living that is in itself godlike, Christlike, divine.

So, my sister or brother, don't eat, don't drink, unless you want to take that risk afresh. Or, if you stay to eat this meal, don't say I didn't warn you. Jesus is contagious, and you probably already have the contagion, yourself.

The Inner Secret of Membership

The planned workshop was still in the offing, but there was very little time to prepare mem-
bers for the serious work we had to do. Our problem, as I saw it, was that we saw membership
in the church (and for that matter, in God's kingdom) as an already fixed fate: those who
were in, were in, but those on the outside would have to remain there. Yet such a view meant
ultimate death for the church; we must grow or die, and evangelism, "gospelism," was our
only effective means of growth. If youth and adult Sunday school classes had existed and
engaged the lives of most members, we might have worked through them to form and reform
attitudes toward the strangers outside and the occasional stranger within our gates. Yet
Sunday school classes were too small and touched too few even of our few. My recourse was the
pulpit, and my text choice was the Letter to the Romans.

Some readers may be surprised by the amount of attention this sermon about evangelism
pays to baptism. Formed by American revivalism, or by a pietism older still, such readers
may have thought that evangelism must appeal for inward faith alone, leaving baptism and
other matters to the churches after evangelism has done its work. A reading of Romans,
though, suggests a different approach. For Paul, baptism was central, not optional or pe-
ripheral. A sociological approach independently yields a similar conclusion: community ex-
ists by means of tangible signs of membership. In other communities these may be lapel pins or
cards for the wallet; they may include initiations or periods of trial membership (as for
fraternity pledges); they may involve the payment of fees or the wearing of a uniform. Yet
there is no reason to invent novel membership signs if we can recover those that are as old as
the gospel itself.

Still, baptism, even baptism shaped by the best historical and archaeological research,
is of little enough value unless its signlike role is recognized, and my goal was not only to

awaken interest in the sign, but even more to look in the direction that it pointed. (Otherwise, the sign itself might substitute for the reality it signaled.) These concerns shaped the sermon that follows.

> What are we to say, then? Shall we persist in sin, so that there may be all the more grace? Certainly not! We died to sin: how can we live in it any longer? Have you forgotten that when we were baptized into union with Christ Jesus we were baptized into his death? By that baptism into his death we were buried with him, in order that, as Christ was raised from the dead by the glorious power of the Father, so also we might set out on a new life.   (Rom. 6:1–4)
>
> [Also read 2 Kings 7:3–9.]

Have you ever noticed how much easier it is for some people to do things? Take hooking a worm onto a fishhook: while the rest of us fumble, uncertain whether we even *want* to do it, the experienced fisherman selects a worm, deftly slips it onto the hook, and look, it is done, ready to lure some lunker trout. Or take gardening. I watch my plants with an eagle eye, yet again and again they die under my intensive care. Yet the real dirt gardener, seeming hardly to look, gives a pinch here, a little fertilizer there, more sun, less sun, more water, less water, and her whole garden is ablaze with color sheathed in green, a joy to the eye and a comfort to the soul. Somehow, she has the knack. There is a knack for decorating, a knack for cooking, a knack for precision toolmaking, a knack for storytelling—a knack some have, some try to get, and some seem never to acquire.

Now this is all very well for fishing and gardening; none of us need do both those things well, and some don't want to do either. Yet what of life itself? What of living the good life, the life Jesus displayed, the life that meets temptation with disdain, endures suffering with grace, answers human need with love that seems to come from God? What is the knack for living such a life? *Is* there such a knack or secret?

Scripture tells us that there is. Today's Scripture takes us inside the workings of God's wonderful gift. Like visitors to some nuclear power plant, here we are taken inside the works, to see how it happens that members of Christ get to be real members, parts of Christ's risen life.

Romans, the source of this sermon, only a dozen pages in most Bibles, is conceivably the greatest piece of literature ever composed. It is about this divine-human secret. What does it say? That the world, for much of its history, has rolled on its course as if nothing ever changed. People were born, lived their lives doing some good things, some bad, and then died. That God was their judge in all this—but where was God? Ah, now comes the central secret. God, says Romans, was present in Israel, readying a people who would change the world; God was present in the old Bible, pointing the way; supremely, God was present in the Jesus story, so that when Jesus' earthly life ended God could say, This was my own life! [See Rom. 1:1–5.] You remember the climax of the story: he was put to death. He was executed by the forces of law and order—no revolutions allowed here. He was executed by the keepers of sacred traditions—who missed the glory dwelling in their midst. He was betrayed by those in his own following—who could not stand alongside him when the going got hard.

Yet (and here is where God-in-the-story becomes most evident), his death was not the end of the matter. Jesus didn't stay dead, didn't stay buried, didn't stay in the past where they meant to leave him. God raised him from the dead; Christ was alive! And that changed everything. For if Christ was alive, sin was no longer in charge of history. If Christ was alive, evil would not have the last word. If Christ was alive, not even death could say no to the good news, the happy outcome, the hilarity that God intended to fill earth's story. And Christ *was* alive; truthful men and women had seen him; Paul had seen him; the church knew him. All that remained was to get the word around. So Paul says in Romans—read it for yourself.

A story from Second Kings illustrates the situation Paul says we are in. Motivated by who-knows-what evil, an army from Syria set siege to Samaria, capital of Israel. This Sarajevo of long ago was near starvation. The prophet Elisha predicted relief, but men laughed the prophet to scorn: Who would save them? Outside the city gates, banished because of their disease, skulked four pitiful lepers. If others were desperate, they were doubly so.

"Why don't we go to the enemy camp?"

"They will kill us."

"Well, but we are going to die here."

So at dusk, hoping not to be seen, the four outcasts crossed the front lines and reached the enemy camp. It was strangely quiet. The four looked more closely; the enemy camp was abandoned! Inexplicably, the besiegers had fled and nobody had realized it. The four darted into a tent, ate, drank, snatched trinkets, ran and buried them, came back to another tent, ate, drank, snatched—and then one said (2 Kings 7:9),

> What we are doing is not right. This is a day of good news and
> we are keeping it to ourselves. If we wait till morning, we shall
> be held to blame. We must go now and give the news.

So they did, and a city that had been filled with hunger and desperation became a city of life and hope once again.

This is the central secret of the Christian community—the enemy is overcome; Christ is alive; your sins are remitted, defeated, banished. Have you heard the good news?

Now the Roman church to which Paul wrote was a mixed group. There were Jews and non-Jews in its membership. There were easterners and westerners. They had different customs, different life stories, different ways of reading Scripture. Yet Paul appealed to what everyone had in common—in those days, all members were baptized. Certainly even baptisms differed. One was baptized in the river Jordan, another in the river Tiber. One was baptized at the seashore, another in a mountain stream, another in a city fountain (Rome was full of fountains). Yet there was something alike in each of these cases. "When we were baptized," Paul writes, "it was a burial ceremony." (See Romans 6:3–4.) "We were buried with him by baptism into death." Not, of course, literal death, but a ceremonial death, a ritual death—to sin. Yet a ritual death so effective that the baptized are now identified with Jesus who died and rose again.

In other words, Romans declares that baptism is a sign, an acted show, reclaiming for the believer the great central event of human history, the death and rising of Christ. Christ died; Christ was buried; that death and burial were the proleptic funeral for sin in the human race. Christ rose, and that was resurrection day for authentic humanity. The question is, how can one identify with that authentic life, that secret of Christian living, Christ in oneself, Christ alive? When the trusting candidate goes under water, he or she reclaims Christ dead and buried. Never again can sin say of your life, "I am in charge here," for the death of Christ has intervened. Your life is buried, interred; what comes up out of the water is a new identity with the risen Christ. The church is the fellowship of the once-buried; the church is the company of the resurrection. Here your old life is buried in the watery waste that preceded creation, *tohu wabohu*. Here your life in faith rises up to last forever—here in dramatic sign is the secret of the Christian life. So far, the teaching of Paul the Apostle.

For long ages these great truths were lost to sight, and the churches suffered their loss. In part this was because churches neglected baptism itself. Baptism was shriveled, diminished, cut loose from faith and from the great story of God's action in the life and death and resurrection of Jesus of Nazareth, cut loose from the repetition of that story in redeemed lives. Baptism then became only a birthday shower, at best a cradle party or a high school graduation affair, pleasant, sentimental, but remote from the risky business of following Jesus in this present age. Yet what God had done remained true, and from time to time through the ages radically Christian churches recovered those facts, written in Scripture, that rang true to the reality of Christian life. A lost secret can be reclaimed. Have we lost the secret here? Do we need to reclaim it?

Baptism, New Testament baptism, is God's signpost, announcing what life (what your life?) is all about.

So what is life, your life, all about? Go back to those miserable lepers who discovered that the invading army had abandoned camp. At least they knew what *their* good news was: the enemy has gone; we need not starve; we can eat our food in peace; we are free, and so is the whole city. Think now, however, of those people inside the city walls who have not yet heard the news. They are liberated but they do not know it. While the lepers gorge on abandoned camp stew, drink whole bottles of abandoned wine, try on abandoned uniforms, the citizens cower inside the city, still terrified. They had heard the prophetic promise—"starvation will end tomorrow"—but they had paid little attention. You can't trust preachers in such serious matters, they thought. They were instead counting out the remaining ounces of flour and searching their cupboards for forgotten morsels of food. Their bellies were shrunk, their throats parched. Perhaps that very night more than one of them would die of starvation. Food, food, there is no food. Yet in truth the enemy is gone; the war is over; the gates can be opened; there is food aplenty.

So is it with all creation. How many are there in this city and this valley alongside you and me who live out pinched, accommodating, bewildered lives, trying for happiness, trying for a good life, trying for contentment, yet still dominated by their own greed or their neighbors' lust, still dominated by the old pride, the old despair, the old hopeless loneliness? For how many is "Jesus" merely a word to use for a mild oath, "God" merely a name for fate, "church" merely a name for a neighborhood clubhouse? Yet all the time that people are believing in these ways, Christ has died and risen; the moral world is made over for eternity; sins, fears, despair are passé, obsolete. If I believed the tidings I have given you this morning (and they are what Scripture says), I would do all I could to live my life in such a way that those neighbors should hear the news. I do believe it: Christ has died; Christ is risen; we are meant to be his members, parts of his own life; that is the secret of the Christian life.

There we might stop, but the Apostle saw another need. There are some inside the church, baptized, knowing full well what God has done, who ignorantly think and live the contrary. These insiders are like those Samarians of old, starving as if God had not liberated their city. So here is the question to these: How can the outsiders who live on *your* street discover their liberation if you who know it, who claim it, who are baptized into it, continue to think and act as if it were not so? As Paul puts it, you have been emancipated, set free, from the old way of life: that is the secret of membership. Have you somehow missed out on the secret?

Two patients were sent by a doctor for testing for a deadly disease. As it happened, neither had the disease, but they could not yet know this. One looked at some papers lying on the technician's shelf. He misinterpreted what he saw and thought it meant he had the disease. The other waited to learn from his doctor that he was healthy. The one who heard the good news from the doctor flourished and lived. The other, afraid to go back to the doctor, sickened, grew worse because he did not know the good news! No wonder we want people to be members; no wonder we want them to seek baptism. Baptism is simply the good news from Jesus the physician. Its message (to those who have ears to hear these words, skin to feel the fresh water, faith to believe God's truth) is this: "Good news! You will not die, but live. You are a sharer in Life itself."

Maybe you have a neighbor, a friend, a family member who is in big need of this good news. Could you not share it? Must you be a greedy leper, gobbling it all for yourself? Or might you instead say, "Come with me to the house of prayer. Hear the good news for yourself. There is enough for you, too. Come, come to the waters."

Born Again?

The struggle for a healthy way of thinking about our inherited faith was far from won. Every sermon preached, every idea planted like a hot ember in the tinder of our communal thinking was a fresh opportunity to set the thought of the church anew upon gospel ways. This next sermon continued the "membership" series of sermons that was to precede our scheduled workshop; it tried to meet head-on the secular scorn some had acquired from the environing culture. It was important to work at this change in attitude, because "new birth," for example, was not an option for us: we desperately needed a new beginning as individuals and as a community. But if we could not even think change possible, how could we be open to it?

There is a deliberate reach in this sermon toward the more intellectual members of the congregation—thus the emphasis on rational arguments and the empirical character of the central illustration (drawn from the Begbie book written early in this century, which is named in the sermon). Where the "baptism" sermon just preceding had emphasized the outward element in a turn to Christ, this sermon emphasizes the inner and psychological element in conversion. One of these is not more spiritual than the other: spirit and substantive action (epitomized by baptism) belong together in Christian thinking.

> "But how can someone be born when he is old?" asked
> Nicodemus. "Can he enter his mother's womb a second time and
> be born?" (John 3:4)

"Born again" means many things to many people. Jimmy Carter, running for United States president in 1976, said he was a "born-again Christian." Four years later, Ronald Reagan announced that he, too, was born again. I missed the announcements about George Bush and Bill Clinton, but surely they accepted the label as well? "Born-again" politics has become part of the American political scene. Perhaps it is a bow to the reentry of "evangelicals" into twentieth-century politics: Pat Robertson, Jerry Falwell, and a host of lesser figures claimed to tell Washington what the "silent majority" was thinking; they wanted to bend power politics their way. With all that, the suspicion arose that "the new birth" is a creature of revival tents, or televangelism for big bucks, or fanatical emotional religion. Many of you know that I take a citizen's interest in politics; I hope you do, too. Yet today I would find it profoundly embarrassing if a political reporter, on hearing that I was a Christian, asked this citizen if he were born again! Embarrassing, not because I do not know the answer, but because if I told the truth I would expect to be misunderstood.

For the truth is that "born again" is not the property of fanatics or show people or office-seekers; it is a plain Bible word with a plain gospel sense. The truth is that this "second birth" is only another way of expressing the meaning of membership. "Born again," or "born from above," is only another way of saying that the Jesus way is a contagious way, so that you are likely to catch it if you stick around. It is only a different way of saying that there is a secret to following Jesus, the inner secret that can merge his story with your own. The truth that I will show you today is that all Christians are born from above, all believers are twice born; there is no other kind of Christian.

The story that will help us understand this is in John's Gospel, chapter 3. A newcomer appears, one Nicodemus. Nicodemus is tentative enough in this shaded night interview: "We know you were sent by God," he begins.

But before we pursue his conversation with Jesus, just who was this Nicodemus? Would it surprise you to hear that he, too, was a politician? "A member of the Council," says the Bible, that is, a political leader charged with the delicate business of maintaining the Jewish state under Roman rule. I hope you think "politician" is a term of praise—it means a maintainer of the *polis,* the humane structure of life together. Don't despise Nicodemus for that! But he is not only a politician, he is a philosopher as well. Look at his answers, look at his arguments: here is no slick street-corner debater, but rather one determined to make sense of whatever there is in the world. I see Nicodemus as an older man, possessed of no little wisdom, rich in life experience—one whose interest in Jesus, the newcomer to Jerusalem, was a full-fledged compliment. Every civilized country has such urbane citizens as Nicodemus, men or women seasoned by life, toughened by the past, ready to size up the current scene and make the best of it. Nicodemus is a worthy inquirer: what will he do with Jesus? And what will Jesus do with him?

The conversation between these two turns on a single question, and it is Nicodemus who asks it. In response to Jesus' saying, "No one can see the kingdom of God unless he has been born again," Nicodemus asks [John 3:4], "But how can someone be born when he is old? Can he enter his mother's womb a second time and be born?" I have heard some people dismiss Nicodemus here as stupid. Has he never heard of metaphor? Doesn't he know about religious language? Yet there is another way to read this text: Nicodemus understands the use of metaphor, and he is using it to ask a wise old man's question: Is there really such a thing as a new beginning in mature life? Hasn't life been fixed by fate, or at least by circumstance, once one's parents are determined, one's education completed, one's domestic life established, one's occupation chosen? You're a young man, Jesus; are you really offering us seasoned old Pharisees a new start? Isn't that rather dreamy? *How can someone be born when he is old?*

Now Nicodemus asked wise questions, but Jesus had wise answers. Let me give in my own words the answer Jesus gave, my interpretation of John, chapter 3. Here Jesus is saying:

> Nicodemus, creation is richer than you think. There is earth with its cause and effect. In pregnancy the infant floats like a swimmer in the mother's amniotic fluid until birth—a first instance of cause and effect at work. Throughout life there is al-

ways cause and effect—flesh gives birth to flesh. But God in Genesis 1 created the earth *and the heavens*—created, in other words, the reality that is conceivable to human beings and the heavenly reality not conceivable to us. It needn't surprise you, Nicodemus, that some things are beyond fleshly calculation: every science has its limits (for an excellent example, think of meteorology); all other human understanding has limits as well. I am talking to you, sir, about that which is beyond those limits, for it, too, factors into created life: One must be born of water— born from a mother's womb—and one must also be born of spirit (that is the reality that transcends our natural knowledge). So, yes, one can be born from above. In your case, the womb of the Spirit must open; God must become a Mother to you nearer than any earthly mother. That nearness, that new beginning, that opening of infinite possibility, will be your true entry into the reign of God. Life isn't ended because you are old; life isn't congealed because you are a politician, or a philosopher, or a business person, or a widow, or a schoolteacher. Life is as free as the wind, the Spirit, that blows!

Thus Jesus spoke, and Nicodemus, we are told, went away. Yet we will hear more of him before the Jesus story ends. Meanwhile, what are we ourselves to make of this declaration by the Master?

Consider the stretch of imagination required to think of "heavenly things" in today's milieu. Is heaven an outworn, mythical idea? It was indeed fashionable to say that, a century ago. More recently, however, mathematicians have explored the possibility of higher-dimension universes, worlds that transcend our own, not by another location "above" or "outside," but beyond our world in another sense of "beyond." One mathematician, named Edwin Abbott Abbott, published a little book called *Flatland: A Romance of Many Dimensions*. In a two-dimensional world, Abbott reminds us, everything is flat. Yet if a three-dimensional world intersects it, there is a bigness, a greatness, that transcends Flatland. Now three-dimensional space matters to Flatland, even though Flatlanders cannot comprehend a third dimension. A sphere, a round ball, passing through Flatland appears there first as a dot, then as a growing circle. As the sphere passes on, the circle shrinks to a dot again and is gone—and that is all of our three-dimensional world that a Flatlander can see. And why, Flatlanders might ask, should there be even this dot-circle-dot experience? To them it makes no sense.

I am not saying that heaven is a higher-dimension world intersecting our own. That is far too easy an analogy. What I am saying is this: When one comes to us who speaks of heaven as if he knew what it meant, when that one is backed by humankind's oldest, longest spiritual tradition—the tradition the Bible records—and when that tradition and that speaking are confirmed by the renewed experience of living men and women for a hundred generations from Nicodemus to today, across continents, across cultures, across all the lines of gender and race and formation, when the knowledge it brings continues to be known without flagging or decay, we need not only to ask with Nicodemus, "How can these things be?" [John 3:9], but must also ask, "Am I, like a Flatlander, missing something central to being human?"

Here we need to draw somewhat upon the church's experience. When does this birth from above come to a particular human being? Is it sudden or sustained? If it is metaphorically a birth, can we even ask how long is the period of gestation, how infantile are its beginnings, how sustained are its consequences? Clearly Jesus is talking about something more profound, higher, than the mere routine of group membership—after all, Nicodemus already had that routine; he was an honored Pharisee. Nor is Jesus merely talking about baptism, though the imagery fits—born of water, the amniotic baptistry corresponding to the birth from above. Nor is Jesus offering a private and inward journey only: new birth, he says, is seeing the *kingdom* (see verse 3) in all its length and height and breadth. How are we to understand all this?

Take the simplest possible case: the church working at the frontiers of human misery. Earlier in our century, one reporter was deeply impressed with the philosophy of William James, who argued that if we only looked closely at the actual phenomena of religion, we would know all of its truth that mattered. The reporter resolved to test the Jamesian philosophy by inspecting religion in one of earth's most difficult settings: the slums of London. With the skill of a Dickens, the reporter pictured people he found living in abject poverty compounded by ferocious human evil—living amid prostitution, organized crime, alcoholism, drugs, social resentment, broken lives stacked one upon another by forces beyond social control. Into that scene, unafraid, had marched the Salvation Army, with its colorful uniforms, its thumping brass band, its settlement houses. What targets these young men and women in uniform made for theft, for raillery, for rape! Yet as the writer began to meet the members of the Army, he found them at ease in this rough setting; many had themselves come from the very streets, the very houses of shame, where now they returned to witness. The reporter, Harold Begbie, told their stories in the book *Twice Born Men.* One by one, Begbie chronicled the lives reversed, made over again, born from above, it seemed—by the witness of the Salvationists to Jesus. Part of the beauty of Begbie's book is its factual character. Not all who came, he notes, were helped. Some who were converted turned back again to alcohol or crime. Yet—here is the real character of the new birth—the Army didn't give up on these failures; with redoubled care it went back to the fallen ones, tended their physical needs, prayed for them and with them, until in most cases the battle was won.

Twice-born men—and women. Is it a marginal phenomenon? I say no. For what Jesus told the urbane Nicodemus has been proved true across the centuries in the lives of a great multitude that no one can number. The birth from above has empirical reality. In some, it is gradual; in some, sudden. In some, it comes in youth; for some, in old age. So the answer of Jesus to Nicodemus' question, "How can someone be born when he is old?" is simply this: the birth from above is the gift of the Spirit who blows where the wind blows, the Spirit who gives birth wherever human life cries out, in Jesus' name, for mercy.

Twice more Nicodemus appears in John's Gospel, first pleading with his fellow political authorities to give Jesus a fair hearing as he himself had once done (John 7:50); later sadly undertaking the task of burying the dead body of the Master [19:39], since Jesus' open followers could hardly risk doing so. This suggests that Nicodemus remained during Jesus' earthly days only a shadowy outsider, lacking the courage or the will to risk everything for the sake of the reign of God. Jesus was right: Nicodemus *did* need a new birth! Yet who is to say what happened after that? The fact that he is so exactly named in the Gospel and never identified as an enemy suggests to me that when the glad Easter news came to others, it came to Nicodemus as well. Then it happened, perhaps, in one more life, that there was a birth from above. I hope so. Don't you?

The Road to Heaven

When we speak of spiritual matters to those in our care, we face a profound and persistent difficulty: how can our hearers be sure that they understand us? During the summer now ending, members had met on Wednesday evening for "food and fellowship," generally followed by some sort of program. On the Wednesday that just preceded this sermon, the program leaders had invited our somewhat reticent folk to speak of their own coming to the knowledge of God in Christ. Ours was not a church in which stylized testimonies set a preexisting pattern. As might be expected, then, the reports we heard were varied indeed. One member spoke of how she had come to a realization of her own faith in praying for an older family member. An older man spoke of the consciousness of a special Providence that had preserved him in wartime. Another spoke of coming quietly and undramatically in the youthful act of entering church membership to acknowledge a faith he felt he had never acquired, but had always had. Several spoke of the more dramatic realization that had come to them at summer church camp, and that at assorted ages. Still another spoke of faith and doubt as continuing partners in her spiritual journey. Another spoke, in a way that made us all laugh, about how "baptism was a big awakening for me"—a theme I picked up in the sermon that follows. Yet another acknowledged summer camp's role, but reported that a later sense of failure as a Christian brought her to the awareness of her need for a Savior. One leader, a middle-aged man, told of a stormy spiritual progress in which faith and rebellion had long alternated.

While I was anxious not to stereotype this rich variety or force it into artificial molds, I believed that I could provide a grid or pattern into which all that our people had reported would fit. That would have the value of showing us to be on the same journey, aimed at the same goal, and presided over by the same triune God. The sermon that follows—once again

*falling on a Lord's supper Sunday—represents my attempt to provide such a biblical grid.
For further development of this theme, readers may wish to read in my volume named* Doctrine *(chapter 3). There the pattern I present is fourfold, in contrast to the more condensed
threefold pattern provided here. While I feel confident that this is a good teaching sermon, I
do not feel equally confident about its homiletical or rhetorical structure—it is one more case
where I wanted a stronger ending than I achieved. Perhaps the trouble once again was attempting too much at a time.*

*Philosophers, by the way, know the question raised in the opening sentence above as the
"problem of religious language": How, in general, can those who speak of God and holy
things understand and be understood? This is discussed in my book with James M. Smith,*
Convictions: Defusing Religious Relativism. *See especially chapters 2 and 3 there.*

> A sense of awe was felt by everyone, and many portents and
> signs were brought about through the apostles. All the believers
> agreed to hold everything in common: they began to sell their
> property and possessions and distribute to everyone according to
> his need. One and all they kept up their daily attendance at the
> temple, and, breaking bread in their homes, they shared their
> meals with unaffected joy, as they praised God and enjoyed the
> favor of the whole people. And day by day the Lord added new
> converts to their number.   (Acts 2:43–47)

This is the last of four sermons on membership—membership
in the church, but also membership in Christ. Now we know membership is contagious—if you stick around here, it is liable to happen to you! Now we know membership comes from a knack or secret, the secret of Christ risen, dwelling in believers' lives. Now we
know that membership is like a birth from above, a new birth. All
Christians are twice born. All *that* belongs to belonging. Yet it
seems to me I have only begun to tell you of the wonder and loveli-
ness of membership in Christ and church. We could fill a book with
it, and last Wednesday evening here some of you said things that
belong in that book. Let me now tell you one more thing: *membership
is a road, and the road has a destination.* I cannot describe that destination very well. But at least let me begin to show you what I mean.

Fifty days after Easter came Pentecost, the outpouring of the Spirit. There the gospel winds began to blow, and they have since spread around the world. You know about Pentecost, for Acts 2 makes it the birth day of the gestating church, and you remember all the stirring things that happened then. Disciples spoke in many tongues, the gospel was preached with awesome power, three thousand were baptized.

We celebrate Pentecost in our services, on one view of the matter, for half the calendar year. Why do we do so? Let me read Acts 2:43 once more, this time in my own translation:

> *Awe* was coming over every living soul, and many portents and *signs* were happening.

We will have to hear more about these signs, but first let me speak about that holy fear or *awe*. This Bible word has almost dropped out of our understanding, and yet it is among the important, elemental words that describe the human relation to God. There is a lower, near-physical edge of awe: in the presence of the uncanny, the majestic, the weird, the hair on the back of one's neck may stand up, one may feel something akin to hilarity or panic and yet neither; these things are beyond our understanding, yet they are a part of human experience. As the pentecostal disciples saw what was happening in their midst, "Awe was coming over every living soul." At its upper edge, awe is the sense of the holy, the divine; when the new Christians saw God's Spirit at work in their midst, their sense of awe awoke; they knew they were perceiving God in their midst.

In our age, and I think in every age, disciples fall into three classes with regard to awe. *First,* there are those who find themselves upon this way but cannot say when or where they inwardly entered it. Awe or salvation is in their lives, but nothing marks their entry.

Second, there are disciples who are lucky enough to know with reasonable certainty when and where they entered upon this awesome path. The Bible says they have *been saved.* Behind them is a fork in the road, and they know that other fork would have led to another destination than theirs; they have turned a corner, taken a new path, entered upon the narrow way with Jesus.

> *Amazing grace, how sweet the sound*
> *That saved a wretch like me.*
> *I once was lost, but now I'm found,*
> *Was blind, but now I see.*

Those who have such memories as these are not better than the rest of us; we might rather say they are luckier—for it stands to reason that if we are on the path, we got on it somewhere. The rest of us just can't say where we got on. In both cases, it is correct to say that we are *being* saved, and that, too, is a biblical way of speaking.

Third, there are those members who have already attained the long goal, reached the destination that "have been saved" and "being saved" both point to. With what awe, what wonder, must such disciples have seen earth's tent poles lifted and cast aside, seen this canvas of our temporal village, this fading mortal splendor, rolled up and stowed away, as a new scene opened before their eyes. Listen to 1 Corinthians 15:54:

> And when this perishable body has been clothed with the imperishable and our mortality has been clothed with immortality,
> then the saying of scripture will come true: "Death is swallowed up; victory is won!"

In Bible language, we *shall be saved* in the end.

Now it makes great good sense to think that these three cases do not represent three separate sorts of Christians, but only indicate three stages along a road that leads from here to heaven. The aware Christian can say, "I have been saved," but can also truly say, "I am being saved," and is therefore in position to say, "I shall be saved." There is the entering stage, the continuing stage, the graduating stage. All are stages on the salvation road, and the happy Christian knows this well enough. The trouble is, sometimes we are not sure where we are along the way. Have I really begun? Am I still on the road? The right road? The first Christians, we read, had "signs and wonders." What signs, what wonders, have we?

So far I have spoken as if salvation were a thing inwardly felt, the sense of awe, the personal knowledge of sins forgiven, weight lifted, God's presence near. And that is not wrong, but it is not all. If salvation is a journey, an actual road to take in this present life, it necessitates visible road signs, markers that all can hear and see, feel and touch. That is what old Alexander Mack, first leader of the small baptist movement in Germany called in this country the Church of the Brethren, realized nearly three hundred years ago. All around Alexander Mack were Pietists who spoke of the believer's inner life. He did not disagree with them, but he wanted more, wanted some road signs to show that his people were on the road, and he found the signs, as had the Anabaptists before him, in the New Testament. What are the signs these pioneers found?

First, for setting out on the way, there is beautiful baptism. Two Saturdays ago, a feature story in the local paper, right next to "Miss Manners," gave a report on people recently baptized here in our valley. As that reporter correctly wrote, baptism is "a sign to the world of the believer's identification with Christ in his death, burial, and resurrection." More interesting to me, since I can get my theology wholesale at the seminary, were the reporter's lively interviews with the recently baptized:

> "Joy was a wreck," Faith says of her sixteen-year-old sister. "But it was a good feeling once the baptism started. It was exhilarating, feeling like we were closer to God. Plus, being dunked like that in the water tends to wake a person up!"

And, this present theologian comments, right on both counts. Here the trail starts; here one does not just feel faith but acts upon it;

one's baptism says, to all who care, "This is me, now—and let God's waves crash over me forever."

This morning, though, the church is ministering especially to those a little farther along. This morning we see the other road sign. It is for those who have begun, all right, but who want assurance that they are on the trail still or once more. And for this need, God has also provided a sign. The hour we first believed is somewhere in the past. Much has happened since. Perhaps there is some sin in your life, and that needs to be forgiven, banished. Perhaps there is some doubt, and that needs to be overcome. Perhaps there is some discouragement, and that needs to be lifted. The dust of the road is thick on your shoes; the sweat of the climb is sticky on your back. You need rest and refreshment. Where did the earliest disciples find it? Listen to the Scripture, Acts 2:42:

> They met constantly to hear the apostles teach and to share the common life, *to break bread,* and to pray.

Is that the way it is with you? Weary, footsore, weak, you come around a bend in the road and look, God has set up a table for you, covered it with a white cloth, and set upon it the elemental food of life. Here is food for the stomach, even if only in symbolic amounts, signifying that God cares about your body. And with it, mysteriously, is food for your soul as well—the risen Christ saying once again, "This is my body, broken for you." This is God's road sign for travelers in the journey's midst.

Finally, what about that road sign at the trail's end? How will we recognize it? How will we know? I can't say from experience, for I haven't been there. I only know that "when he appears, we shall be like him, for we shall see him as he is" [1 John 3:2]. Will that not be a time of awe, of wonder? Certainly. But so was baptism, and so is this awesome feast that awaits us here today. In fact, what we do now is a foretaste, a moment of anticipation. We look at this bread and wine, and by faith we see the great supper feast of the Lamb. We look at the faces around us and see—not just Jim and John, Ruth and Nancey, and all the others—but faces destined to be like his face. In the end, all the rest will fade away, and that one face, the Master's face, will remain. He tells us he will be with us, then as now. That will be heaven indeed.

The Word

The next sermon explains its own context so well that not much need be said about it before-hand. In theory, we were a "people of the Book," Bible readers and Bible believers; in practice, we had left Bible study aside and had not gained or kept the skills to make ourselves Bible readers once more. Thus an obvious avenue of growth—enlisting newcomers in the pleasant intimacy of Bible study classes for all ages and circumstances—was closed. I hoped to reopen it, and hoped that the now imminent workshop might provide a mandate to do so.

That is the context, but the sermon does more than point a way toward needed church action. It also provides, in brief, a point of view toward the Bible as a living, active partici-pant in our common life. I hope it may be a point of view that appeals to readers as well.

The Spirit said to Philip, "Go and meet the carriage."

(Acts 8:29)

Last week saw the signing of an accord between the State of Is-rael and the Palestine Liberation Organization, guaranteed by the nations of the West, at a historic meeting in Washington, D.C. Leaders who had continued a century-old war between the peoples of the Middle East met to begin a new chapter in history. Muslims, Christians, and Jews promised to work together for peace. Adopting an American phrase, they pledged to "give peace a chance."

On the night of the signing, my wife and I sat up long in bed watching the televised ceremony with eyes sometimes damp with tears. One feature struck me with special force. As they tried to match their words to the magnitude of what was happening, Jewish and Arab and American leaders quoted the Bible—other sources certainly, but again and again the Bible. Here, it seemed, was a book that could make sense of history. So once again references to Isaac and Ishmael, to the walls of Jericho, and to the haunting biblical call for peace on earth gave resonance to human speech.

On a different scale, in a different sphere, our church faces a historic moment in its journey. We have suffered loss of momentum and loss of a pastor, setbacks in the church's life. We have wondered whether our setback is fatal—whether the vacant pews, our increased age, the growing fatigue of some who have carried the burden so long are too much for us, or whether these bones can live. Together we have asked, and soon we will meet in an all-important *workshop* to thrash out the answers. Our "recovery room" season is ended. Now we must act, if we are to be a real church. The question now is, what must we do? *What is our mission?* Just how are we to be a church? Will it surprise anyone that in our own crisis of history, our own strategic agreement will focus on the Bible? If worldly politicians know these pages, must not the church of Jesus Christ know them? Yes, we do know that our health, our mission, is bound up with these pages, and that we must find a way to make God's Word central to our mission once more. Today I hope to show you that way.

Someone may object that the Bible is not lost at all. Everyone is familiar with it; it is the all-time best-seller of all books; every bookstore has it; every family owns one or more copies; every hotel room has a Gideon Bible in a drawer. And I agree that these things show that people recognize the importance of this book. Why else would we buy it, and give it to others, and stock hotel rooms with copies right next to the local television guide? It seems we know it is important. But do we know what it says? If someone asked you what the Bible is about, could you tell him or her with assurance? What *does* the Bible say about honest business practices? About love and sex? About sickness and sorrow? About children and their upbringing? About who Jesus is? If we hesitate, is it because we are not sure

where to put our feet down on biblical ground? Unsure, that is, just
how to interpret this Book of books?

Why is this so? How is it that in a nation of many churchgoers,
almost no one can interpret the church's book? What we cannot understand, we will not read; consequently the uninterpreted Bible is
an unread Bible. I mentioned hotel room Bibles. Have you ever seen
one that looked used? And for that matter, what of the inside of your
own Bible?

It would go too far afield to report the experts' explanations of
this American biblical illiteracy. It has many causes—the individu-
alism of modern life, the cultural shift that took place in the century
now ending, the failure of seminaries to make good teachers of their
graduates, and still more. We can ask about the causes another day;
now we must ask how we can become Bible interpreters once more.

Today's text is a story of Bible reading that provides the key to
all Bible reading. Philip, an evangelist, has been sent down the Gaza
road. (This is the same Gaza as in current news from the Near East.)
Though afoot, Philip is offered a ride by a visiting financier who sits
reading in the back seat of an elegant vehicle, much as if a hitchhiker
were to become a passenger in a stretch limousine. Before long, financier and hitchhiker are deep in conversation, for the first question of Scripture reading has been asked and correctly answered:

> Philip: Do you understand what you are reading?
> Passenger: How can I without someone to guide me?
>
> [Acts 8:30f.]

This is the opening key: We *must* read the Bible with someone prepared to guide us.

Philip's conversation brings us to the very center of biblical interpretation. The passage under examination is Isaiah 53:7–8. The
limo owner, who is from Ethiopia, says (Acts 8:34): "Please tell me
who it is that the prophet is speaking about here: himself or someone else?" Then, the text tells us, Philip started from that passage,
and told that Ethiopian financier the story of Jesus.

Oh, someone will say, how lucky that the financier happened to be reading from a classic Suffering Servant poem in Isaiah. That made it easy for Philip. Yes, but don't you see that there is no place in Scripture, no place at all, that does not lead on to the story of Jesus? Scripture is many stories, utterly human in their fabric, each deeply moving in its own right. Yet the golden thread that links them all together is the story of God—the story of what God is doing to make human life humane, of what God is doing to draw people to himself.

> *Genesis* is the story of beginnings—not only the beginnings of earth and life, but the beginnings of a people who might lead all people to God.

> *Exodus* is the story of how God delivered that people from slavery—the beginning of the liberation that Jesus came to continue.

Skipping along, the books of

> *Samuel* and *Kings* tell how the people wanted a king and a kingdom—which could only work if God was King in the different kind of kingdom Jesus would proclaim.

> *Psalms* is the hymnbook of the coming kingdom, when all creation will praise its Maker and Redeemer.

> *Isaiah* is the voice that declares the character of a people fit for that coming rule. And passing over all the books that explicitly name Jesus, come to the very last: *Revelation* announces the final triumph of the Lamb, the Prince of Peace, whose cross is the cost of God's victory on earth.

So the Ethiopian treasurer asked the right question: "Who is it that the prophet is speaking about?" And Philip the hitchhiker gave the right answer: "Starting from this passage, he told him the good news of Jesus" [Acts 8:34]. That is the key to the Bible.

We must not leave out the character of Philip's student. He was a distinguished person, a high African government official who had attached himself to the biblical story even before he met the evangelist. He was intelligent, competent, discriminating. That is the sort of Bible student we must watch for, be ready for, the sort that the Spirit of God may lead us to. On the other hand, this student, whose destiny was to be the model Bible student, was disadvantaged: His castration (following a harsh custom) made him an object of disdain; his color made him with all like him a victim; his alien status made him marginal. And again, such students are the very ones we must seek to recruit. It is not enough to say we do not discriminate: We *must* discriminate to find the marginalized, bring them in, open the doors of faith to each one.

So the church has a mission with the Word of God. It has the key to interpreting this Word: that key is Jesus. It has prospective students—the distinguished who are marginalized, the Word-hungry marginalized, who will come to us when they learn that we are ready to receive them, prepared to teach them, formed by this very Word as servants of one another and of Christ.

Notice one more thing about the mission of Philip the hitchhiker. It has a practical focus. Philip interpreted the Bible in such a way that the financier wanted to become a follower of Jesus just as Philip was:

> "Look," said the eunuch, "here is water: what is to prevent my being baptized?"
>
> [Acts 8:36]

And so they had the chauffeur stop that stretch limousine right there in the desert, went over to the oasis in a roadside park, both waded out into the water, as was needful if Philip was to baptize him. He did, and a brother went on his way, "rejoicing." When the Bible is truly taught, Bible readers want to do what it says.

What, then, is our mission? We are to be a people of the Book. That is true of our origins—the earliest members of our movement were Christians who knew that they could recover their heritage only if once again they became a people of the Book. That is true of all the peoples that have made and been made by this book, this

Bible. Only if we are a people of the Book are we children of the Author of the Book; only if we are a people of the Book are we followers of Jesus, the center of the Book. But how do we become such a people?

We must begin with the Sunday school that is already in place. This is now minimal, but it means that those who are laboring now do not labor in vain.

Beyond that lies a wider plan: New classes, new teachers, new students, ones not now enrolled in Sunday church school and not now attending our other services, but who, like the traveler from Africa, are distinguished yet disadvantaged, people of every age who want to understand the Book, yet cannot unless someone guide them. As a start, I envisage a Sunday school of one hundred members. How will this happen? From our gifted membership and friends we will *recruit new teachers.* These will not be teachers to divide up the students in present classes; they will be recruited to teach classes not yet in existence. We will *train* the teachers, guiding them in the style of Bible teaching that Philip the hitchhiker employed when he met the traveler from Africa. Then we will *create new classes* by discovering people who want to learn, and we will use our new teachers and helpers to *visit and enlist* these students. Finally, our classes will not be mere dilettante sessions, not places for folk to gather and gossip, not places to air opinions and prejudices to one another; they will be working sessions that will issue in *discipleship.* They will lead on from Bible study to prayer, from Bible study to witness.

❖   ❖   ❖

Will it work? Skeptics say that the Bible must remain in a hotel room drawer, unopened and unread. Skeptics say that people don't think being Christian is worth much work. Skeptics say that our church must fail and die. *God says otherwise.* Why is this story here, in the Book of Acts? Not just to tell a story of long ago, not just to show how it all began, but to show how it can continue in every Christian generation. If the Bible tells the truth, there are those in our generation hungry to read the Bible, to pray, to witness. We can find them, we can teach them; we can and we will. That is God's message. It is our mission now.

The Witness

The sermon that preceded this one was the first of three that (as our workshop expressed it) pointed up the three major tasks our church faced, its three major reasons for existing. It lived to proclaim the word of God, yet also to constitute a living witness to that word, and finally to worship God in prayer and praise (see the sermon after this one).

Thoughtful readers will realize (as thoughtful members of the congregation certainly did) that these are mutually inclusive categories; to be true to themselves, each interpenetrates the other two. The church's witness is treated here as a matter of good works, and I will explain in a moment why it is. Yet surely the church's witness also includes the proclaimed and taught word of God. The Bible is a book of witness if it is in place in the life of the church. And surely, too, the church's worship is a witness-in-prayer to the same God whom the church serves in word and works? In fact, it is just this interchangeability of terms that tells us we have found the right terms indeed. What we have is not a church of three duties but a church of one duty. "One thing is needful," the Master once said to a faithful practitioner of the way of works (Luke 10:41f.). What, then, is that one thing? Jesus does not say, and the underlying thesis of this sermon, with the one that precedes and the one that follows, is that if we understand word and witness and worship correctly, we will see that each names it, each shows an aspect of the one thing that disciples are required to be about; that one thing is also called faith and eternal life and salvation!

Thus the conversation that in this sermon takes place in the homeless shelter could serve as an illustration in the preceding or the following sermons as well.

There is a reason for the order of these sermons. The witness of good works came easily, almost naturally, to our people; this sermon was meant to encourage, praise, and reinforce their existing practice. On the other hand, the preceding sermon on Bible study put forward a challenge. So I intended a rhythm of demand and reassurance, now urging, now encouraging, in sequence.

> . . . and you will bear witness for me.   (Acts 1:8)
>   [Also read Isa. 58:5–11; Matt. 25:31–46.]

It is common these days for businesses, universities, and government agencies to formulate a "statement of mission." This tells the business, the university, the agency its purpose. I suppose children's curbside lemonade stands also have mission statements; it seems the thing to do. "We exist to sell lemonade to grownups!" So these sermons on mission, of which this is the second, are very much the style.

In one way, the church's mission is different from all other missions. For we have the Scriptures. We are a people of the Book. And in the Bible we find both precedent and mandate for our own mission. Let me call your attention to a central statement: After Jesus had risen from the dead, he appeared to the apostles during forty days. And then, in Acts 1:6ff.,

> they asked him, "Lord, is this the time at which you are to re-
> store sovereignty to Israel?" [In our terms, this might have been
> "Lord, are you going to make ours a great church this very sea-
> son?" To which he replied:] "It is not for you to know about
> dates or times which the Father has set within his own control.
> But you will receive power when the Holy Spirit comes upon
> you; *and you will bear witness for me* in Jerusalem, and throughout
> all Judea and Samaria, and even in the farthest corners of the
> earth" [not excluding this city and this valley in Southern Cali-
> fornia, U.S.A.].

There you have it. The mission—the apostles', and therefore our own—is not setting up God's kingdom. It is not even achieving success, as the world of businesses and universities and lemonade stands reckons success. The Christian mission is completely stated in that one phrase, calmly put forward not as a command but as a prediction: *You will bear witness for me.* When is the church the church? Not when it adds many members—though growth is good; not when the church makes all its members happy—though joy is a gift from God. The church is the church, the church fulfills the mission set once for all by Jesus himself, when the church witnesses for the risen Lord Jesus Christ. That is our task.

We need to be clear about the idea of witness. Our best secular example is a witness in a courtroom. If you watch courtroom dramas on television, you know the rules. The witness is not the attorney, hired to make arguments. The witness is not the judge or jury, deciding the outcome. The witness is the plain citizen who comes to the stand to tell what he or she knows. Fancy lawyers (at least on television shows) may try to trip up a witness; rival witnesses may contradict; legal arguments may discredit. But the good witness simply declares what he or she knows—the truth, the whole truth, and nothing but the truth.

This is the way it was in Scripture as well. Once Jesus gave sight to a man blind from birth onwards. The enemies came and tried to trip up that man's witness. Isn't it this or that instead? they asked. But the man who for the first time could see had a sufficient answer: "All I know is this: I was blind and now I can see" [John 9:25].

The original witnesses to Jesus testified not only with their words, but with their lives. Hear Acts 2:42: "They met constantly to hear the apostles teach (that was the witness of the Word) and to share the common life (that was the witness of their deeds, living like Jesus lived), to break bread and to pray (that was the witness of faithful worship)." Original Christianity was not chiefly a matter of talk or of ideas and opinions; it was a matter of a new life, a new way of life, together. Jesus had shown the way; God had confirmed that way by making Jesus Lord and Christ; now the way was open to all, and witnessing was not just talking about the way, but taking it. As a wise saying has it, God has retained very few of us as attorneys, but has summoned all of us to be witnesses.

Now someone may disagree with this: According to the record

of early Christianity, didn't the apostles go *preaching* the word? Didn't Philip explain the Scripture to the Ethiopian traveler, showing him Jesus at its center? Didn't Paul and his fellow missionaries go into the synagogue in every new city preaching Christ? Wasn't proclamation at the center of early Christianity? Yet the answer is quick at hand: indeed they did, for God's original people, Israel, already knew the way of life Jesus exemplified—knew it, however well each followed it. They had the Ten Commandments; they had the Law; they had the lifestyle taught by the prophets. What Israel then lacked was the openness to the new tidings that came in Christ, news that God had opened a new stage in Israel's history, so that the business of the prophetic missionaries was to tell them the story of Jesus—the new thing that God had done for them and for all.

Yet that did not cancel the importance of taking Christ's way and living it. Again and again, in writing to his new converts, Jew and non-Jew alike, Paul insists that those who know the good news must, like the faithful men and women of old, submit their entire lives, not merely their words, to God. Romans 12:2:

> Conform no longer to the pattern of this present world, but be transformed.

And Paul goes on in that passage to outline the contents of a life of witness—see his list of gifts from verse 6 to the end of chapter 12.

Now let me put this as a question: If that spoken message was the chief need of the first-century people who needed Christ, what is the chief need of the residents of this valley? What witness do our friends and neighbors need? I expect that every resident of our valley, even the most isolated, has heard the name of Jesus. "Jesus Christ" is a common, mild swearword; it is also the name of some churches and of some denominations; it is also the common explanation of what the gospel is about—namely "Christ"-ianity! I hold before you a page of the local paper: it is a long list of churches offering to witness by talking, talking, talking. Our own church ad is here on this page, also, and my name is on it, promising that we, too, will talk! But where among all these advertisements is the church that promises to witness by doing, doing, doing?

Let us be honest: this church does its share of talking, and it should. Last week's sermon, "The Word," made that clear. Where we and others must differ, if we do differ, is that we are convinced that the witness of talk is hollow until it is matched by the witness of deeds, the witness of character. For what we *are* will speak so clearly that others cannot hear what we say—cannot hear it, unless what we say *matches* what we are.

Yet in this realm of deeds the witness of our larger denomination and the witness of this congregation ring clear. Our fellowship has a sterling record of meeting human need at home and abroad. One small example is the program called "Alternative Christmas." The sponsors, working through missionary contacts in Two-thirds World countries, buy up inexpensive handmade products of great beauty and value. These are brought to us, and on a November afternoon here you will be able to purchase these gifts—alternatives to the conspicuous consumption of the shopping mall Christmas spree. Christians elsewhere prosper, and your gift is itself a witness to the true meaning of the birth of Jesus—a new way of life breaking into the world.

Other forms of witness are even closer to you. Almost twenty years ago, facing a growing regiment of folk out of jobs, out of luck, out of home, radical Christian leaders in this city, some of them members of this congregation, began a shelter in the downtown where those folk in need could find a meal, a friend, a night of indoor sleep. The number in need has grown: So where does such a project find staff? Part of the answer is found in this church. Sturdy cooks in our church sign up to prepare and serve an evening meal for sixty or more hungry, hurting children of God. Last Wednesday it was our congregation's turn once more, and our leader let me come along for a look. Twenty minutes after arrival I had learned to make coffee in an urn and was permitted to stand in the cafeteria line putting a slice of white bread on the plates of sixty-four "customers"—the meal is free—while other helpers dished out our chief cook's macaroni casserole and tossed salad, food good enough to make me hungry. After their meal, I sat down to talk with one guest, there for the first time. Here I will call her Jacqueline.

"Are you going to convert me?" Jacqueline asked shortly. (So much for the reputation of the ministers of the word.)

"Well," I said, "maybe you are going to convert me—what do you believe?"

"Oh, I believe in Jesus," she replied firmly, "but I need a counselor; I was abused, and I can't get away from the memory. My brother is a rich lawyer, but he won't help me, won't even listen to me."

Too bad, but I believe the shelter ministry is going to help Jacqueline. One who has worked often at the shelter tells me that when she stays as an overnight resident she regularly meets people who want to talk about Jesus, talk about the Bible, talk about God—and about their own broken lives.

Someone will ask if the people at the shelter deserve to be helped. Do they deserve these free slices of white bread and tossed salad and macaroni casserole? I am sure that often they do, but that is one question Jesus never asked. When at the end of the world the King sits upon his glorious throne (with all the angels) as the nations are gathered for judgment, he will say to those on his right hand:

> You have my Father's blessing; come, take possession of the
> kingdom that has been ready for you since the world was made.
> For when I was hungry, you gave me food; when thirsty, you
> gave me drink; when I was a stranger, you took me into your
> home; when naked, you clothed me; when I was ill, you came to
> my help; when in prison, you visited me.   [Matt. 25:34–36]

And when they admit that they have no memory of doing any such things for him, the King will answer:

> Truly, I tell you: anything you did for one of my brothers [or sisters] here, however insignificant [that brother or sister seemed],
> you did for me.   [Matt. 25:40]

That is what the King will say, but it appears he will say nothing at all about whether those so-called insignificant brothers and sisters were deserving, or worthy, or were themselves righteous—nothing at all. That seems not to enter the calculation. The truth is, we are doing it for the King—and *he* is worthy; it is enough.

There is one more thing—you are invited to sign up for a turn at the shelter, yourself. Ask any of our deacons, male or female; they will see that you get a chance. Maybe they will give you the honor of handing out the bread. Moreover, you don't have to be a member of this church, or of any church, to go. And I believe that fact is one of the keys to our church's future. For there are folk in our neighborhoods who want to be helpers, but don't know how. A part of our evangel task is enlisting those who would be servants of God in the army of the Servant-King.

❖ ❖ ❖

What we do at the shelter is a way of witnessing—taking our place on the witness stand for Jesus. Christianity is faith in Jesus. It is also, and equally, that very faith acting—faith showing hospitality, faith sharing, faith healing, faith forgiving, faith making peace. I have to tell you one other thing, though: Witnessing is costly. If you follow Jesus as a witness, you are as a matter of fact spending your life, expending your life. The word "witness" in our text is Greek *martus*. From it we get the word "martyr." A martyr is simply a witness, and every witness to Jesus is of necessity a martyr as well—one who has surrendered not some things, but everything, to Jesus. Hence I must be honest with you: Faithfulness to Jesus may quite literally cost you your life; it has happened often enough in our times. In a broad sense, faithfulness to Jesus is sure to cost you your life. Whether you die on the mission field or die at home in bed, you are a martyr, a witness, if you follow him. So I invite you to follow, but only if you have considered the cost!

The Worship

The all-church workshop met, and it was a success. Most active members came and took part; by day's end on the workshop Saturday, we had together formulated a mission statement, which, among other things, took into account the threefold pattern I had been urging. Thus this sermon, on the following Sunday, was in position to lay in place an exposition of this third corner of our mission statement.

Concerning worship (as it had been with reading the Bible), the big obstacle was a lack of primary Christian skills. The difficulty in this case, though, was not being out of practice; it was instead flawed practice, based on undesirable models. All America was shaped by an entertainment model of worship. What was to some degree true of all was supremely true of us Southern Californians living, as we did, in the heartland of the entertainment industry. Our people, like others, turned on the television or went out to see movies or shows; there someone got up in front to make them gasp or laugh or cry. Or our people went to church, or to interchurch rallies, and as far as the leaders could manage it, the same thing happened. Preachers told jokes; they encouraged their "audiences" to reach out and shake hands or slap one another on the back; they related touching stories evoking maudlin sentiment; and good, fuzzy feelings followed. But God remained a spectator. Another model was provided by our neighbor Catholic and Orthodox churches, yet they had their own problems, and in any case they were too remote from our people in other ways to be in position to share their distinctive good with us. We would not become good baptist worshipers merely by imitating nonbaptist ways, though almost anyone could have taught us better than we already knew. In such circumstances, could we even discover the high, holy doctrine of shared prayer that was our own proper heritage?

I resolved to avoid sermonic scolding, but as far as possible to encourage true worship by setting verbal pictures before the congregation that would supplant, perhaps eventually erase, the old, misformed pictures. With it all went the hope that we might together offer our weekly prayer so as to reach out to the strangers nearby—not to entertain them, but to evoke from many a hurting breast the publican's prayer: "God, be merciful to me a sinner" {cf. also 1 Cor. 14:24f.}.

> Here is another parable that he told; it was aimed at those who were sure of their own goodness and looked down on everyone else. "Two men went up to the temple to pray, one a Pharisee and the other a tax-collector. The Pharisee stood up and prayed this prayer: 'I thank you, God, that I am not like the rest of mankind—greedy, dishonest, adulterous—or, for that matter, like this tax-collector. I fast twice a week; I pay tithes on all that I get.' But the other kept his distance and would not even raise his eyes to heaven, but beat upon his breast, saying, 'God, have mercy on me, sinner that I am.' It was this man, I tell you, and not the other, who went home acquitted of his sins. For everyone who exalts himself will be humbled; and whoever humbles himself will be exalted."   (Luke 18:9–14a)
> [Also read Isa. 6:1–9a.]

The trouble with this parable of the two worshipers in the temple is that for us it has lost its punch. Translated, the parable goes something like this: there were two church members, one whom nobody admired and one whom everybody admired. Both went to church; both prayed; the guy everybody liked was a flop at prayer; the guy everybody despised got through to God. Now *that* is a parable: it tweaks our prejudices; it makes us think again. I am afraid, though, that for a long time in the churches the good guy of Jesus' parable has become a bad old Jew, and the man his hearers would regard as the bad guy has become merely a model Christian. In that event, the parable as we read it has lost its sting: it reinforces our prejudices rather than challenging them, and we miss Jesus' point.

So let's start over, set aside those two characters, and try a different story, not a parable in this case. Imagine an overseas business visitor to our city, imagine a woman in the midst of a painful divorce, and imagine a child of the church, too old to march out with the little ones, but too young to keep listening to a twenty-minute sermon. Now please ask which of these, coming to our church this autumn Sunday morning, would find his or her way to God in prayer? In this revised story, the burden is not first of all upon the new arrivals—the businessman, the woman, the child—the burden is upon *us*. Is that not right? Is it not our mission to be the church in such a way that any of these might not only come to church, but also come to pray? Can we be such a church that here men and women and children will meet God? I say that we can, and that hidden within Jesus' parable is this home truth for us.

Jesus takes it for granted that people want to pray. The two who in his story come to the temple have no other intent. Both want to pray; both know that the house of worship is a place of prayer; both come intending to pray; both invoke the one God. Yet their prayers do not equally meet with success. Now this offends our sense of propriety. Surely, says liberal religion, prayer is a human prerogative? Surely I can pray when and where and as I please? And surely God has to hear, has to answer, has to forgive? As the old French proverb has it—that's God's *métier*, God's business. But Jesus' parable says it is not so—the one worshiper went home justified, and not the other!

So our first assumption must have been mistaken: all things are not equal; one prayer is not as good as another. And come to think of it, why should it be? Little that is human is unlearned. We begin human existence equipped to breathe air, to suck milk, to cry for help, sometimes loudly, and little else. Our other skills are minimal. We learn to talk by imitation; we learn to walk with considerable help; we learn manners and cooperation and self-sacrifice only by way of painful lessons. Why should it be otherwise in our walk with God? Human understandings of God vary, but (as my friend and former student David Keyes reminds me) no great religion expects its adherents to come to the point of its teaching without instruction. The Zen master may require you to sit in silence for a year before instruction begins. The rabbi may demand that you learn Hebrew—after all, it is the language God speaks. Jesus summons disciples and asks them to follow him through thick and thin. Why are we here today so different? Or do we imagine we have a natural gift to know without learning, to understand without paying a price?

What, then, of the visiting businessman, or the victim of divorce, or the preadolescent child of our own parable? Why, they are welcome to come here—as welcome as the prodigal son coming home—but they will surely need help. And here we come to the point of what we do in church: Our worship is prayer; its focal center is prayer; its end is prayer. For prayer, true prayer, is encounter with God. It is not merely so many words launched like a rocket into spiritual space. Rather, prayer is meeting; it is our answer to God who has first spoken to us.

Now we begin to see the point of worship. *Worship is the framework of practice in which we may respond to God.* We want to pray, but we do not know how. God through the church gives us a setting; God puts words into our mouths, so that here we can learn how to pray and can take the lesson home.

Yet worship is not merely instruction—if it were that, there would be something else beyond worship to which it was only a stepping stone. There is not. Rather the goal, the end, is here in our midst; this divine-human encounter itself is the prize. After a day's conversation about it in the workshop just ended, you characterized our church as "an intimate 'family' relation in Christ." I think "family" is indeed a clue. One need not live as a family member to come to this church, but living with family or housemates may give some hint of what worship realizes.

I am at home, and someone else is there, also. I cannot see or hear her, yet I know she is there (probably upstairs, working), and if I did not know she was there, the house would feel different. In my case, it feels oppressively empty. Better still, sometimes she and I are in the same room. Perhaps we do not touch or even speak, yet her presence is unmistakable and delightful. Finally, it is day's end, and she is with me in one bed. The sign of Jesus' presence, however, is not connubial but more elementary still: He is present with us in the waters of baptism that surround us like a refreshing bath; he is present in the elements of the holy meal we share, present in the food and drink that enter us, elements that become ourselves, feed us, turn finally into our own bodies. He is present, literally, when we pray.

Is it any wonder, then, that the true church of Jesus Christ rejects the *performance* theory of worship? Worship is not a performance, says the editor in chief of the hymnbook in the pew before you. There is nothing wrong with performance, of course. I love the movies and the stage; I even like television, sometimes. Yet worship is altogether other. Here we come, not to see a show but to meet Jesus, not to be delighted but to be forgiven, not to show off before God and our fellows (that was that Pharisee's mistake) but to be seen by eyes that will see us and see through us at the final trial.

What then of our business visitor, our woman recovering from a broken marriage, our child looking to grow up? What can we offer them in this meetingroom? We can help them to discover a presence here, a Christ risen, a Spirit hovering, a God who will be to them more than family. Was it not the defect in his own family relations that led Jesus to call *God* Father?

What are we to do, then, when we come together here on Resurrection Day, the day the world calls Sunday, as promised? What is to be the shape of our shared worship? Certainly we must frequently repeat these great remembering signs—baptism, prophetic preaching, and the Lord's supper—that are ordained signs of God's presence. Certainly we must pray explicit prayers, for prayer is our answer to that holy presence. And assuredly we must sing, for music expresses the power of what we sense and say here. But in what order shall we do these things? Just as the old Anabaptists, seeking to recover the ancient practice of believers baptism, sought out the most ancient form of that rite and gradually discovered the form we share here now, so we want to repeat the pattern of worship nearest to the

New Testament. Thus we look back to the earliest paradigms: Jesus meeting the disciples after the resurrection, the earliest missionaries meeting in private houses, the earliest churches of which we have record. What pattern appears?

It began, in those days, with baptism. The disciples found a river, a city pool, a country pond, and in the waters of baptism they washed one another as Jesus washed their sins away. How many have followed since! So worship even today begins with baptism whenever we have a candidate. Baptism is Israel, standing on Jordan's banks and looking over to the Promised Land; baptism is John, dipping his soiled countrymen and women in that same Jordan with his cry, "Repent!" Baptism is Jesus, baptizing "at Aenon, near Salim, because water was plentiful" there [John 3:23]. Baptism is Paul, getting himself immersed in Damascus where he had meant to immerse the church in persecution. Baptism is rank upon rank of martyr Christians, who, unable to fulfill the baptismal command, were "baptized" in their own blood in the continuing persecution. Baptism is myself, a boy standing long ago in a baptistry in faraway Louisiana and making promises that are good to this very hour.

Worship continues: after we baptize, we listen for God's proclaimed word. We read from Old Testament and New—first from the Old, for it is God's ancient word to his people; then from the New, for it tells the story of Jesus. We hear the preached word, uttered in the Spirit, heard by courtesy of that same Spirit, so that these words of clay and spittle spoken in this or that homely accent and with this or that preacher's finite gifts become to us listeners words of life and light, showing what the Spirit says to the churches.

Worship soars: Next follows offertory, when what we have, our gifts, our lives, are brought before the Lord. We give our offerings of money. We lay our joys and sorrows before our Redeemer. We converge in concern and lay out the witness to the week begun.

And now the climax: Worship feeds upon God's feast in the meal of memory and hope. This comes last in our worship as it came

last on the night in which Jesus was betrayed, when he took bread
and gave thanks and broke it to share.

> *And thus that dark betrayal night*
> *With the last advent we unite*
> *By one blest chain of loving rite,*
> *Until he come.*   {*George Rawson*}

The supper is Jesus anticipating Calvary; the supper is apostles part-
ing for life-threatening witness in unknown lands; the supper is our
own ancestors meeting in Asia or Africa or Europe and certainly in
the Americas to take our places in a line two thousand years old and
more; the supper is ourselves, gathered in sickness and in health, in
joy and in sorrow, in good times and bad times, but always nurtured
by the One who gave life that we might live. The supper is that One,
who lived and died for us and rose again.

So worship proceeds from baptism to the word to the climactic
eucharist. What of the times when we have no candidate to baptize?
On those Sundays at the beginning we say words or repeat gestures
that recall baptisms past and future. We hold its place. So it is with
the supper. When we come to the end of offertory, the gifts are
brought forward, hands are lifted in prayer, and we remember that it
is mealtime for believers, even though on a given Sunday the visible
signs are absent. So the pattern remains the same week by week, and
when, as I hope will soon be the case, we have all the remembering
signs regularly in place, our prayers will be unchanged, but
complete.

What, then, of our businessman, our woman, our child? How
will they pray, when they come to pray with us—for all worship is
rightly prayer. Of course, it depends upon each of them. But our
hopes for them are high, as we remember that ancient businessman,
the treasurer who came to Jerusalem, and returning home sought
help from Philip the preacher—sought it, and received it: "Then
they both went down into the water, Philip and the Eunuch, and he
baptized him," and the Ethiopian, distinguished but disadvan-

taged, "went on his way rejoicing" [Acts 8:38f.]. Our hopes are high, for we remember that woman of many marital disorders who met Jesus at the well, and, hearing him preach a sermon created just for her, exclaimed, "Where can you get 'living water'?" [John 4:11]. Our hopes are high, for we remember what Jesus said when children pressed near him: "Let the children come to me; do not try to stop them" [Mark 10:14]. And, type of them all, there is the unloved bad guy in Jesus' parable, who prayed (Luke 18:13), "God, have mercy on me, sinner that I am." Our mission here is to enable such prayer; our mission is to pray such prayer. That is our worship.

Bound for the Promised Land

Participants in the successful workshop had made plans, but these needed to be turned into concrete performance if we were to become again a vital congregation of God's people. I felt I needed a narrative to make this marching sermon vivid; perhaps we would sing "I'm Bound for the Promised Land" in the service in which it was to be preached? Once again, then, the narrative would come from the exodus story, this time from that retelling in Deuteronomy in which Moses calls a halt to the wilderness wanderings (important enough in their own right) and announces a fresh word from the Lord: turn north toward the Promised Land.

My task was made easier by an image our workshop's professional "facilitator" had offered us: at his instruction we had begun on that significant Saturday by forming small groups, each provided with paper and crayon to draw a "picture" of our congregation conceived as a motorbus with its passengers. Clever group members had depicted our church's plight in various ways: with a flat tire, without an engine, with no door through which anyone else could get on board. The pictures had made it easy to talk about the good and bad in our church's past and present. These homely drawings were still fresh in our minds, and I could evoke them toward the beginning of the sermon.

Theological readers will recognize this sermon as an application of an important principle mentioned elsewhere in this volume: the approach to biblical interpretation I call "the baptist vision." In more traditional language, this means that Scripture is applied typologically: The events and circumstances of the biblical past form an image of the life of the present community so that the biblical message becomes ours. In this case, the command to march north becomes our command to take up the new tasks of our "promise" or covenant from the workshop.

One of these was a project to reach out to students in the local seminary, especially

overseas students who had no regular church home here. We would do this by inviting them to
a free meal.

> Then the LORD said to me, "You have been marching round
> these hills long enough."   (Deut. 2:2–3)
> [Also read Acts 13:13–20; 32f.]

Israel had learned to live in the hills. People had come to like the
out-of-doors. At first, there had been grumbling and protest—some
even wanted to leave the wilderness and return to Egyptian slavery.
Yet here there was a new life, and most had come to like it. They had
their herds; they had meat to eat; some even planted grain on the
hillsides so that there were crops to harvest. Everyone had a tent,
shelter from the desert sun and rain. Most who were now alive had
been born in these wild hills and had come to consider them home.
They moved often, their future was unclear, but home is home.
There was just one problem: Israel went round and round and round
the hills and got nowhere. And then, as in their grandparents' day,
there came a fresh word from the Lord: "You have been marching
round these hills long enough; turn northward."

Now that command was frightening to the Israelites. Why, they
had heard that in one of the countries they must pass through there
was even a king who slept in a bed nine cubits long (a giant, no less!).
Great kings, fierce nations, deep Jordan waters to cross. What they
did not see (though Moses must have seen it) is that while indeed
there were dangers ahead, there were now skills, after these forty
years of wanderings, that would suffice for the journey. They had
learned to trust God. They had learned to live together. The law
taught them both these things. On a humbler level, they had
learned to live simply, out in the open; they were tough travelers,
hardy desert folk, ready for what the future might bring.

I suggest to you that this passage describes our church. We cannot turn back; there can be no return to our sweet, remembered
past. At present we circle among the hills of difficulty: our "bus" has
flat tires, or no engine, or rolls over a bumpy, uncomfortable road.

And yet, the word has come like a marching order from God: we must make a new compact; we must discover our promise from God and God's promise to us and our neighbors in this valley; we must be (these are your words) a *"fellowship that seeks to meet individual needs . . . to develop in ourselves and others an intimate 'family' relation in Christ"* calling forth *"commitment to our heritage of word, witness, and worship."*

Brave words! What makes them realistic words is that they are based on God's own promise and command—and that they are based on the skills we have learned these forty years, the things that we do and do well. Like Israel of old, we have learned in the hills how to make our way home.

Take the matter of studying God's word. There can be little doubt of its importance. Shared Bible study always pulls God's children together. Primitive Israel, escaped from Egypt, had no library of scrolls, no Bible, not even a single book of the Bible, but that quickly changed. Moses ascended the mountain and came back with two flat stones on which were written the guidelines for keeping their promise: no other Gods, no empty oaths, no deceptive idols. Positively, keep God's holy day, inscribed in time, and keep God's holy future by teaching children to honor parents. All the other essentials of their new way of life followed these: no murder, no adultery, no theft, no lies—and do it all with all your heart. For these were the Ten Commandments, Ten Words to live by. They could read—it was part of their Near Eastern heritage to be a literate people—and when they broke camp, Israel loaded the stone tablets of the law into an ark or box, for they must not leave their charter behind. Of course, the Ten Words did not long stand alone; around the originals a body of law and custom collected, and this collection continued growing, until they had the Law, the Prophets, the Writings—all that today we call Old Testament or The Original Promise. (And beside this, Christians, thanks to Jesus and his apostles, have a New Testament, a New Promise uniquely inscribed for us.) Without both Old and New we would be no people, yet we are a people of God, and these books are our constitution, our deed of title.

We have this book, and we have our new *commitment.* Two of its items are:

- communal Bible study
- one small-group meeting (at least one for each of us)

Let me interpret this: It means that those already doing so must continue, and those not yet doing so must begin, to meet regularly with others in a small group that takes the Bible seriously as God's written word to us. For most of us, that will mean that Sunday school can no longer be merely for little ones, or merely for those with an insatiable desire to go to one more meeting (a desire I try to resist if ever I feel it). One way or another, each of us must take part in shared Bible study.

We cannot make these changes instantly: Some new groups must still be created, and the special needs of special individuals can and will be respected. Yet we are on our way. Today a new young women's class was launched. Another teacher is at work on a class for youth. A third has spoken to me of a class for women who cannot meet on Sunday morning because they teach others. All these things will happen; there will be a place for you; and this because God says, "You have been marching round these hills long enough."

Many good things happened to Israel while they were marching round and round among the hills. Families learned to make camp together. Children learned how important it was to obey their parents. Herdsmen learned to ranch, and farmers learned to sow seed in the wild desert hills. Just so, many good things have happened to this church during the forty years since this building was occupied. High among them is our long-standing practice of witness: the meeting of human need. I cannot enough sing the praise of those who have offered hospitality, visited the sick, opened the checkbook to those in need. Even in these long years of circling the hills, this church has been forming skills that will be needed in the Promised Land ahead. Let me give you one small example.

Alternative Christmas is a plan for bringing handicrafts from poorer mission lands to *this* mission land, to sell them on an appointed Sunday after church. The money goes to support our less able fellow Christians, the gifts to remind giver and receiver alike that Christmas is about a different kind of gift. Each year we do this, and we do it well. We have the skill. Now, however, I want to suggest a new step forward: Let us *advertise* Alternative Christmas in a bold way in the media, notifying outsiders both of the sale and of the service that precedes it, so that it will draw to our church outsiders who want to find a new approach to Christmas, who yearn for a new approach to living. Such advertising requires some thinking; I put it forward as a proposal.

Next, consider another plan in the making. On the first Sunday in November this church proposes to provide luncheon for those new seminary students and their families in our city who will accept our invitation. The cooks in our congregation are sure to prepare a stunning meal—they always do, and I plan to be at the table, as I hope you do. But what will bring students to such a service? Well, one of our members who is professor in the nearby seminary has procured a list of new, unaffiliated students. (We don't want to steal others' sheep!) Another member, wearing I suppose her printer's smock, has created a beautiful invitation, to which one of our church visitor cards will be clipped. These will go out in the mail, and deacons have agreed to phone and make the invitation personal so that we can anticipate the size of the crowd. Finally, that particular Sunday will see us in one of our most attractive settings—the chapel eucharist—and I believe most who come to our Seminary Feast will want to come to church beforehand as well. You will need to find your place in all this, and (not least) you will need to be on hand in chapel that First Sunday morning, with bright smiling face, ready to welcome guests who may wish to return.

These things are both old and new. For us, the skills are old. We acquired them while circling the hills—round and round again—as we learned about Alternative Christmas, as we learned how to put on a church luncheon. Now our marching orders have come, and these old skills come with us. Thus God says, "You have been marching round these hills long enough; turn northward."

Another commitment, you said in the workshop, is

*   *regular worship.*

Let me interpret this one for you as well. Why do we come here, Sunday by Sunday, and take our places together? Why does one member stand like a welcoming angel at the church door? Why do other members usher and take the collection? Why are our liturgists, our readers, our children's storytellers faithfully in their places? Why am I here, and our music leader and organist and choir members in their places, rehearsals done, gowns donned, ready to do their part? I say it is because Jesus has taught us to pray, to come together and pray.

Now that seems to some a foolish answer. Why, these will say, I can pray at home; I can pray in my car on the freeway; I can pray on the golf course. And of course that is true; people can pray in all those places. They can and they do: many a golfer hits a hook or slice, and then utters a prayer, although I am not sure God cares very much about answering. For what we all need, golfers or not, is to learn to pray as we should. James 4:2f. [KJV]:

> Ye have not, because ye ask not. Ye ask and receive not, because ye ask amiss.

"Teach us to pray" [Luke 11:1], the disciples begged Jesus, not because they had never prayed or knew no prayers, but because they believed he knew the secret of happy prayer.

Let me put it differently. We yearn, all people seem to yearn, for an intimate encounter with God. We want to touch the source of our being. We want to be forgiven. We want the vector of a life fit for reality. We want these things, and coming to church, we find them. Music touches our lives and fills us with the passion prayer demands. The faces of friends remind us of the love of Jesus. The great, God-given signs—baptism, prophetic preaching, and the Lord's supper—speak a language God is teaching us, signs in which we communicate with the risen, present Christ. Listen, for example, to the Greek Orthodox instructions for Holy Communion:

> *As thou dost approach, O mortal, to receive the Body of the Master*
> *Draw near with awe lest thou be scorched: It is fire.*
> *And when thou dost drink the Holy blood unto communion,*
> *First be at peace with those who grieve thee,*
> *Then with courage receive the Mystic Food.*

Now why am I telling you these things? For you know them. You have already made "regular worship," that part of our new Promise, the habit of your life. When you are within driving distance of this place on the Lord's Day, you are here without fail, as is right, and you are careful not to put yourself beyond driving distance without grave need, for you know that you have a covenant to keep, a tryst with the Eternal, an intimate encounter to make good. You will not fail your divine Lover, for the Lover will not fail you. We have learned all this in the wilderness, these forty years, as we circled these same hills, round and round.

Yet now there is a new command: You must think of another. It is no longer enough to be here, but you must be praying that God will lead you to those whom you will invite, saying in effect: come tryst with us; come learn our speech; come sing our music; come witness with us these mighty signs. And so to us God says, "You have been marching round these hills long enough; turn northwards"—to the Promised Land.

❖ ❖ ❖

Will we already be in the Promised Land when we do these things? When we bring along our friends? When we serve the Seminary Feast? When in our groups we read together God's written word? No, the journey will be longer still. There are dangers ahead; there is Jordan to cross.

What will it be like, that Promised Land, when we do see it? How will we know we are there? Perhaps we cannot yet say. What we do already know is this: God is ahead, a pillar of cloud by day and a pillar of fire by night. Continue to circle these dry hills if you like, but God's people in this place are bound for the Promised Land.

The Ghost Story Jesus Told

For once, Halloween, October 31, fell on a Sunday. The old missionaries to northern Europe (in the fourth, third, and perhaps even the second centuries) had encountered Halloween's predecessor, a collection of quite terrible practices, and had tried to overcome them by providing a substitute celebration, All Saints' Day, November 1. Nevertheless, Halloween had persisted, and had come to America with European immigrants. It was a measure of the degree to which ours remained a pagan culture that most citizens of our valley were well aware of Halloween (and some went to elaborate trouble to decorate their houses and instruct their children in its street rituals), while relatively few were conscious of the intended Christian supplanting holiday, All Saints' Day. Our church stood with the many, not with the few. What, then, should the preacher do about this calendar fluke, Halloween Sunday?

Our church did not observe all the secular holidays, and not all the Christian ones, either. Yet this pair of secular and Christian days seemed too good an opportunity to let pass—and a chance to preach on a wonderful text that offers to correct the moralism so many mistake for Christianity.

It is one of the sad ironies of this particular Halloween and All Saints' time that on that very evening, youths in our city shot and killed two innocent children in the street on their way home from Halloween activities. Child sacrifice was by no means at an end, and this grisly event reminded us, as we thought back to it, of still other ways in which our culture sacrificed some of its children. How urgently the city needed the church, and how urgently we needed to learn to make gospel sense of the world in which we lived. Perhaps a little tug toward a renewed Christian All Saints' Day might not be out of order.

"When an unclean spirit comes out of someone it wanders over the desert sands seeking a resting-place; and if it finds none, it says, 'I will go back to the home I left.' So it returns and finds the house swept clean and tidy. It goes off and collects seven other spirits more wicked than itself, and they all come in and settle there; and in the end that person's plight is worse than before."   (Luke 11:24–26)

[Also read 1 Sam. 28:8–20.]

Halloween is fun. It is also a lot of trouble for parents—candies, costumes, trick or treat. Nevertheless, we keep on, year after year. How long *have* we kept on? Well, there was Halloween before there was Christianity in northern Europe—and that means before A.D. 200, 300, or 400! If your remote ancestors were German, Irish, or Scots, they were pagans in that long-ago time. The pagan harvest festival came every November 1st and the night before. It was a fearful time. Bonfires were built to encourage the sun to keep burning through the dark winter ahead. The old Scots used to say there were *ferlies* abroad in the countryside—gods, wonders, ghosts, hobgoblins. On that pagan night and day the boundaries between worlds were considered erased, spirit-beings visited earth again, and evil things were done. Sometimes human beings were even put to death as a sacrifice to placate the visiting gods.

If we want to explain our Halloween, we have to recall Christianity coming north. To replace the deadly November rites, the missionaries began the month with a day of All the Saints—All Saints' Day, November 1st. The night before was All Saints' Eve, in Old English, All Hallow's Eve, or Hallow Evening, or Halloween. Despite the missionaries' efforts, some of the ancient customs continued—among them dressing up in supernatural costumes and going from house to house to receive propitiatory sacrifices from householders. These old customs came to America with Scottish and Irish immigrants. And so we have in our valley not the pagan Celtic Samhain, but its successor, Halloween. Still today, many here keep

Halloween who never heard of All Saints' Day. For belief in ghosts, demons, spirits—such beliefs are persistent in humankind. In Old Testament times, King Saul once consulted a witch—proving to the biblical writer that Saul had lost his trust in God. Even Jesus told a ghost story, once. Why he told it you will soon see.

First, the story. Once upon a time, there was a haunted house. It was almost empty—only one demon lived there, but I suppose one demon is enough. No doubt there were creaks and groans and strange lights and ghastly smells—all you would expect from a real demon. The owners decided something had to be done, so they called the demon-removers and had their house de-haunted (you can do that, you know, or at least in Jesus' story, you could). Now the demon, evicted, had to look for a new place to live, and went to many real estate offices and investigated many abandoned warehouses and old shacks, but nothing seemed right. One night, though, while out ghosting, the demon happened to go by his old residence and discovered that it was still empty. Not only that, but it had been beautifully tidied up. New paint, new draperies. The demon grinned demoniacally. He went around that very night, collected seven demon buddies to move in with him, and the last state of that house, said Jesus, was worse than the first.

Luke has told Jesus' story in such a way that we cannot miss its point: The house is a human life; the demon is some evil thing that possesses that life; the owner gets rid of the evil, but fails to replace it with anything else, whereupon the old evil and much more return to haunt that life.

Why would Jesus tell such a story? Certainly not to make us expert demonologists. Every Christian generation seems to spawn a few such experts (there are some around the seminary where I teach!), but it is no part of Jesus' program here to encourage belief in supernatural beings called demons, or to discourage such belief. Some people nowadays would have you believe there are in fact such beings. Others say no. I'll tell you the truth of the matter: I don't know. Explicit demon possession is indeed a widely reported phenomenon. I think, however, that it makes no difference whether this is a matter of actual "spirits" clutching at human life, or whether it is instead a matter of "mere" psychology. The things that happen, and the tragic outcomes for human life when they happen, are real enough in either case. People do find themselves possessed, their souls invaded, their lives involved in evil beyond their control. They give way to drugs or to alcohol, or to the influence of some powerful person, or some gang or club. Why it happens doesn't matter now; that it happens is a fact.

The point of the haunted house story is that expelling evil influences is not enough. Of course these need to be banished. Of course we yearn to be free from crippling dependencies, destructive life-patterns, demon ghosts that flit through our lives, deposit their guano in the secret places of our selfhood, ruin our closest human relations, sour our spirits. John Bunyan, that seventeenth-century chronicler of every pilgrim's progress, wrote a more personal book, *Grace Abounding,* in which he told of his own inner struggles. Listen to a passage from it:

> [If a sin] were to be committed by speaking . . . such a[n evil] word, then I have been as if my mouth would have spoken that word, whether I would or no. And in so strong a measure was this temptation upon me that often I have been ready to clap my hand under my chin to hold my mouth from opening; and to that end also I have had thoughts at other times to leap with my head downward, into some muck-hill hole or other, to keep my mouth from speaking.

In such times of compulsion we need exorcism, de-haunting, cleansing. Joyfully, Bunyan at last found that God would take his compulsion away. But that was not enough, because the old dependencies, old patterns, old ghosts—and more like them—will inevitably come back to haunt again.

So what is the answer?

The answer is present here in the story. It is present throughout the entire Gospel of Luke. It is exactly empty houses that attract ghosts; it is exactly the empty life that risks possession by another spirit than the Spirit of Jesus. That is why "a house swept clean and tidy" is not enough for any of us. The vacant house attracts ghosts until it is filled with new occupants; the life that is cleansed of a false dependence is in peril until that life is taken up with a new loyalty.

Don't you know how it is with love? When a love affair finally, irrevocably ends, when you break up and your heart is broken, what is the cure? Nothing helps like a new love. Only in finding a new interest do we overcome an old heartbreak. And the same is true in all life. A good habit replaces a bad one, faith in what is evil can be replaced only by taking up true faith. Horace Bushnell called this principle "The Expulsive Power of a New Affection."

Who is it, then, who must fill the house of my life if I am not to be haunted by the old ghosts, old demons, old dependencies, so painfully ejected? The answer is: the Storyteller himself. It is Jesus who told the story of the haunted house; it is Jesus who offers to come and make his home with you. Hear his summons in Revelation 3:20:

> If anyone hears my voice and opens the door, I will come in and he and I will eat together.

Do you remember the old gospel song:

> My Jesus, I love thee, I know thou art mine . . .

It continues:

> For *thee* all the follies of sin I resign.

The point is that if your house, your life, is empty, you need not be alone. Your life may be haunted by habits you do not want, but it will not be enough to give them up. It will not be enough to de-haunt your home place unless another, a "thee," this Jesus, this storyteller guest, is brought home to live with you.

"Swept clean and tidy"—that's just the way things should be for a guest, don't you think? Only we need to be sure that the invitation is extended, be sure the guest we really want coming to our house is actually invited. Otherwise "clean and tidy" may be not an invitation to happiness but only to disaster. "Swept clean and tidy"—but don't wait too long, don't spend too much energy on barren self-improvement, mere self-reform, or else you may miss the coming fun the saints have always known. You need to let Jesus come into your life, and thus to become a part of the oldest community of faith on earth, reaching from Abraham to Israel to the church of Jesus Christ.

In every generation, that faithful church faces demons. In such times, we have on our side not only God and God's Christ and God's Spirit; there are also God's people—that "vast throng, which no one could count, from all races and tribes, nations and languages, standing before the throne and the Lamb" [Rev. 7:9]. Today is the eve of All Saints' Day. Tomorrow is the day in which through a long history the church of Jesus Christ has celebrated its sainted membership. For a moment, then, let us recall them, and not our current demons. Let us recall the saints on earth as they appear in the mind's eye of the Christian poet:

> *But lo! there breaks a yet more glorious day;*
> *the saints triumphant rise in bright array,*
> *the King of glory passes on his way.*
> *From earth's wide bounds, from ocean's farthest coast,*
> *through gates of pearl streams in the countless host,*
> *singing to Father, Son and Holy Ghost, Alleluia, alleluia.*
> {*"For All the Saints," W. W. How*}

When the Fire Burns, Where Is God?

Southern California is a region blessed with a very mild climate, with winters that are the envy of much of the rest of the nation, and with wonderfully accessible surf, sand, and mountain snow. Yet the region was not designed for the large metropolitan population that has moved here in the last century. In particular, houses in Los Angeles County have been built far up into the chaparral-covered canyons that spill out into the grassy plain—spill devastating flood and fire at certain seasons. With our earthquakes, these features make the local climate an exciting one, to say the least, and a devastating one for the unprepared. I was at a doctor's office across town on the morning referred to in this sermon; when my wife phoned that danger loomed, I raced across town, and together we wet down our shingle roof with a hose, watched the nearing cloud of black smoke with anxiety, and prepared to evacuate if the firefighters failed. As it happened on this occasion, the wind fell off and the fire was turned about half a mile from our residence. Others did not get off so easily.

Here as in other parts of the world natural disasters raise questions in Christian minds about the sustaining providence of God. This is not the "problem of evil" so dear to philosophers of religion since the time of Leibniz, King, and Hume, a "problem," as I have pointed out elsewhere, that works from a false standpoint and cannot hope to obtain satisfactory results (see my Doctrine, 171–76). The questions that naturally rise in believing minds, however, are serious enough, and deserve pastoral care of the sort represented by this sermon.

Readers interested in theological ethics may recognize the three divisions or spheres in which God works and we respond ("nature," "culture," and "tomorrow" in the sermon) as the strands of Christian ethics picked out in my Ethics: the organic, the social, and the resurrection strands.

I do not believe in apologizing for sermons or for cooking: my rule is either don't serve it or don't apologize. Still, we ought to be aware of our weaknesses: I never found the strong conclusion I had wanted for this sermon. Nevertheless, I believe it works, and so I include it here.

> There he entered a cave where he spent the night.
> The word of the LORD came to him: "Why are you here, Elijah?" "Because of my great zeal for the LORD the God of Hosts," he replied. "The people of Israel have forsaken your covenant, torn down your altars, and put your prophets to the sword. I alone am left, and they seek to take my life." To this the answer came: "Go and stand on the mount before the LORD." The LORD was passing by: a great and strong wind came, rending mountains and shattering rocks before him, but the LORD was not in the wind; and after the wind there was an earthquake, but the LORD was not in the earthquake; and after the earthquake, fire, but the LORD was not in the fire; and after the fire a faint murmuring sound. When Elijah heard it, he wrapped his face in his cloak and went out and stood at the entrance to
> the cave.   (1 Kings 19:9–13a)
>   [Also read Rom. 8:18–39.]

When fire burns, where is God? That is what people want to know. When the earth quakes, where is God? When the great rains come, and rocky debris slides down the canyons, crumbling houses, pouring deep mud into city streets, where is God then?

For us, these are not idle, speculative questions. In the morning darkness of Wednesday, October 27th, two weeks and four days ago, in the canyon two miles upwind from this church a homeless vagrant started a fire to keep warm. Most of us woke to very hot wind—and the sound of sirens. By midmorning, dwellings on both sides of the canyon had been destroyed and the fire had leaped both south and west. Some of our congregants prepared to evacuate, and had the wind not died down, it is likely that many of us would be as homeless as that homeless soul. Meantime, across California sixteen other major forest fires, fanned by the same Santa Ana winds and fueled by the same dry, oily chaparral, threatened wildlife, houses, and people. In acres burned, one of these was seven times our fire; in structures destroyed, only two exceeded our own.

Many of these, including the deadliest fire, were set by pitiful, malicious human beings, arsonists. Curiously, that does not keep people from asking about God's role in those very fires. Couldn't God by a miracle stop the arsonist? Or at least stop the fire from burning as far as my street?

I want to answer, want to show you where God is when the fire burns, but to do so I must ask you to listen to the word of God in Scripture. If you will not learn the biblical answer, I can be of little help to you. But if you want to hear God's answer, you must understand that God is not only the God of *nature*—God is indeed that— but also the God of *culture.* And not only the God of nature and of culture, but also the God of *tomorrow,* whose costly future is nonetheless known to us in Israel, in Jesus, and in the beckoning church of Jesus Christ. Until we put our question, "Where are you, God?" to the real God, we will have no real answer. When we do hear the real God, and get our answer, we will find we also have a mission. Come fire or flood or deadly plague, that mission must go on.

A curious thing about our recent fires is that there is something strangely attractive about them. The awesome sight of all those tons of underbrush and trees and even houses bursting into flame draws spectators. The fire is terrible, but it is also fascinating, in a way we are somewhat ashamed of. The television crews knew that, and they filled our screens with blaze, even when we might have been better helped by less sensational maps and information. Fire is much more absorbing to watch than decay, even though, chemically speaking, it is the same thing—oxidation. The truly perverse watcher is the arsonist, the crazed individual who watches the fires he has set.

Have you considered, though, that God the Creator is an "arsonist," too? To create a universe in which rapid oxidation is possible, to generate the worlds by fiery suns, to form earth's crust over molten lava and perforate it with volcanoes, to grow forests in desert climates and send lightning that ignites the dry wood—are these not cosmic arson? Go out into the desert at night and look up; what do you see? A billion fires, burning to form the worlds. God likes fire, too.

Of course, to say "arsonist" twists the point, for the Creator's fires come not from malice or insane pleasure, but as part of the whole order of nature. We sing of God's rule in the Pentecost hymn, "Wind who makes all winds that blow," but also, "Fire who fuels all fires that burn." Those lines are about God's Holy Spirit, and refer to the wind and the flame on Pentecost Day, but they also speak a more general truth, as illustrated in Hebrews 12:28f.:

> Worship God as he would be worshipped, for our God is a devouring fire.

The very nature with which we are surrounded in Los Angeles County is a fire-loving nature. Our rainfall in some years is no more than that in the Gobi desert. Here organic matter does not rot. The chaparral grows on the steep slopes of our San Gabriel mountains and builds tons of dry growth per acre per year. Naturalists say that before human beings dominated this area, there were fires every thirty years or so, returning the organic matter to the earth as fertilizer so more could grow. Many mountain seeds do not sprout until heated by fire to six hundred degrees Fahrenheit. Perhaps many years go by, then the fire comes, life returns, and nature's ecological chain continues. Listen to journalist-author John McPhee [*The Control of Nature*]:

> All chaparral has in common an always developing, relentlessly intensifying, vital necessity to burst into flame. In a sense, chaparral consumes fire no less than fire consumes chaparral. Fire nourishes and rejuvenates the plants. There are seeds that fall into the soil, stay there indefinitely, and will not germinate except in the aftermath of fire.

Or listen instead to God's word in Genesis 1:31:

God saw all that he had made, and it was very good.

When our kind came upon this western scene, we built fire roads, slowed the rate of fires, and consequently the dry fuel builds up—hence the big fires including our recent fire. At the same time, we (or our developers) built frame houses in Eaton canyon, in Malibu canyon, in many another dry canyon, surrounded by fuel, unprotected by open space. When we do this, God does not alter the rules of the universe. How could he? They are the very thing that makes nature work.

Very well, you will say, but has God forgotten us, God's human creatures? What about us, when the fire burns? Where is God then? Surely the first answer is that *God is there in the fire.* God sustains all nature, keeps it as nature, and does not in the regular course of things turn it into something else. Christ does not change the temperature at which wood ignites; the Creator does not change the urgent need of chaparral to burn; the Holy Spirit does not install firebreaks around new housing developments in this county. If God changed the facts every time we ignored them, the universe would be a crazy place: fire would not always heat; food would not reliably nourish; water would not quench thirst. Life on earth would fail. We need a dependable nature. Without it, we would not have a habitable world.

God has not forgotten us in making nature stable, but we may have forgotten where God is to be heard. We can learn a good deal about God and the weather by reading the Elijah cycle in the books of Kings. At a time of great personal discouragement, Elijah fled to Horeb, the mount of God. Surely, here, God would tell the prophet what was in store for him. Now Elijah was accustomed to God's speaking in the fire: once fire from heaven had fallen on his sacrifice, defeating the prophets of Baal. So perhaps when Elijah came to Horeb he expected God to speak in the fire. But what happened?

First came the wind, "rending mountains and shattering rocks," but God, says the text, was not in the wind—not there, that is, with a message. Then the earthquake, but the Lord was not in the earthquake. Then at last came fire. Surely God would speak by fire? But the Lord was not in the fire. After the fire came "a voice of gentle stillness," as one translation puts it. Then Elijah knew to listen, and he went out to hear God's voice.

How has God spoken to us in the days just past? Perhaps God spoke to some people in the fire, reminding them of past folly, warning them of wrath to come. Certainly the fire suggested to me and Nancey, my wife, that we need a fire-resistant roof over our hillside home, and when we can we are going to get one. But I think the voice of God was not mainly in the fire. I think it sounded most clearly in the quiet, courageous work of those who cared for us all in the crisis. I am thinking of firefighters, some of whom came from far away to help. They were God's gift in a time of need. I am thinking also of a story in the local paper, based on an interview with people whose house was surrounded by the wildfire:

> When we were getting ready to leave our home [a woman told
> the reporter], my two sons got down on their knees, facing the
> fire, to pray to God to save our home. I called a friend to ask her
> to pray for us, and she said she would pray that God would send
> guardian angels. [When] we left—the fire was within three feet
> of our car. [When I came back afterwards] the fire had burned
> right up to the door. There was a guy putting out hot spots, and
> he wasn't a fireman, so I went up [to talk to him]. I told him
> about my friend and he started to laugh. Then he told me *he* was
> a member of the Guardian Angels [a local group of volunteers].

There were many such stories, whimsical and sad, heroic and ordinary. People helped one another in magnificent ways. A member of our church lives on a street that was in the direct path of the embers. He spent that terrible Wednesday organizing his neighbors, helping the elderly, wetting down rooftops, and keeping his neighborhood safe. That member was God's "voice of gentle still-ness," only a "faint murmuring sound" compared to the roar of the fire, but a voice that said, We are your brothers and sisters, we care about our neighbors, we believe in God, we will help you if you need help. We are willing to be your guardian angels in time of need.

❖   ❖   ❖

Where is God when the fire burns, or the earth quakes, or the floods with their rocky debris descend? Well, God is in the fire, in the wind, in the rocks themselves—God is God of all nature, and God keeps nature being nature. If we forget that, if we think we can ignore nature, do as we please, and expect the Creator to bail us out again and again, we are going to be surprised. The second, deeper lesson, though, is this: God speaks in the voice of gentle stillness. What God said that day to Elijah on the mountain was not what Elijah had wanted to hear. Elijah had wanted God to send fire to destroy evil Jezebel. Elijah had wanted the priests of Baal burned alive; he had done his best to destroy them, himself. Elijah had wanted a God who would rule the world by violence. It was not to be. God, in the voice of gentle stillness, said, "Go home and anoint Elisha to be your successor!" Now Elijah was a prophet of terror, while Elisha was a powerful but gentle human being. In effect, God was saying: "The day of terror is over. Once, Elijah, I had to speak by fire, but no more. Now I will use the gentleness of Elisha; your fiery prophet days are done."

Sometimes, surprising as it may seem, the gentle voice of Scrip-ture says the truth better than any of us can do it. Let me read once again, at sermon's end, what Paul in Romans 8 [22–29] says on this very matter. Will you let God speak to you here as I read?

> Up to the present, as we know, the whole created universe in all its parts groans as if in the pangs of childbirth. What is more, we also, to whom the Spirit is given as the firstfruits of the har-

vest to come, are groaning inwardly while we look forward eagerly to our adoption, our liberation from mortality. It was with this hope that we were saved . . . and in everything, as we know, he co-operates for good with those who love God and are called according to his purpose. For those whom God knew before ever they were, he also ordained to share the likeness of his Son, so that he might be the eldest among a large family. . . .

Enemies

I pointed out in an earlier introduction that one of the features of our small church was the Love Feast, an evening in which there would be a time of devotion, the ritual washing of feet, and a simple communal meal of soup and bread, climaxed by communion. Twice a year we observed this simple rite. As it happened, we had not done so since the departure of the alienated former pastor and the rancor and estrangement that upheaval and crisis had produced. Other events had intervened: there had been a sort of group therapy session, in which the former pastor and his wife returned by invitation and sat with the rest of the community for a time of reconciliation. In my judgment, that event had been moderately successful in healing the breaches that still existed. One family (I regret to say) simply left, and began to attend another church. For the rest, there had been a gradual diminution of tension as we focused on the way forward. One keen observer in the congregation, a woman who had been there a long time, told me that whereas formerly in the coffee hour after church people talked in little groups to one another, now there was more general socializing—the separate groups seemed to be merging into one. I took that as a good sign.

The Love Feast, though, was a time when our internal dissension would surely keep some at home if reconciliation was not real and deep. Part of the service was a short devotional talk at the beginning, and it would be my task to give that talk. I decided to use a message that I had given once before, in the earlier case to a nonbaptist Christian congregation at their eucharist. Perhaps it would work in these circumstances as well. Though we were moving forward, now, it would be good if the wounds of our recent trouble could at last close over. I decided to try.

The Dirk Willems martyr story (which does indeed have a very grim ending, as martyr stories do) can be found in Martyrs Mirror.

You have heard that they were told, "Love your neighbor and
hate your enemy." But what I tell you is this: Love your enemies
and pray for your persecutors; only so can you be children of
your heavenly Father, who causes the sun to rise on good and bad
alike, and sends the rain on the innocent and the wicked. If you
love only those who love you, what reward can you expect? Even
the tax-collectors do as much as that. If you greet only our
brothers, what is there extraordinary about that? Even the hea-
then do as much. There must be no limit to your goodness, as
your heavenly Father's goodness knows no bounds.

(Matt. 5:43–48)

Love your enemy! Does it make sense? Note that Jesus didn't say,
"Have no enemies." I could have understood that, I think. Indeed, it
is this world's wisdom. If enemies appear, waste them, trash them,
get rid of them. Or if you can't do that, smile, and pretend they aren't
enemies. Admittedly, this elimination of enemies never works out
very well. The smile is hypocrisy; your enemy usually sees through it
and is even more your enemy than before. Though we imagine violence actually removes enemies, the long experience of the race
shows it isn't so. The enemy will turn out to have allies; after your
deathblow is struck, you will have more enemies than you did before. No, the truth is, you can't get rid of your enemies, and those
who try make havoc of their own lives. As Jesus put it, all who take
the sword will perish by the sword [Matt. 26:52]. So Jesus doesn't
say, "Have no enemies"; he knows that in this world you will have
them. But *love* them? Who can honestly do that?

Some have done it. In the sixteenth century there lived a Dutch-
man named Dirk Willems. He was an Anabaptist, which as everyone knew then (and most still believe today) was a very naughty
thing to be. Moreover, Willems permitted his fellow Anabaptists to
have meetings in his house. So the authorities hired a thief-catcher, a
sort of contract cop, and assigned him the task of catching and ar-
resting Dirk Willems. But being warned, Dirk fled—across the ice

of a frozen Dutch canal. The contract cop (in this story, he *is* the enemy) followed. Dirk had gotten safely across the canal when he looked back to see that his pursuer had broken through the ice and could not climb out. He was surely going to freeze to death. So Dirk Willems turned back, and rescued his pursuer. As the story is told in the old Anabaptist book *Martyrs Mirror,* the thief-catcher would have let him go then, but the town mayor called out to insist that he arrest Dirk, who was of course nonviolent and did not resist the arrest. So he proceeded to arrest Dirk Willems and bring him in.

Clearly this was a case of "love your enemy," and that not in the sentimental sense but in the practical sense of doing him good not evil. Yet when this story is told, or for that matter when Jesus' command, "Love your enemies," is seriously proposed, I think two reactions follow from most hearers, or at least most Christian hearers. The first is a rather wistful, "Yes, there is something right about that." The other is the feeling that all the same, it can't be done, generally. Now I'm not saying I could have done it. Dirk knew what a risk he was taking, and I assure you things were not nice for him after his arrest. Yet it is interesting that this story is told and retold in the Anabaptist community to this day (and similar stories are told among Franciscans, among Quakers, and among others who take this command of Jesus seriously).

The point is this: what we cannot do if we were simply on our own, we can do, can acquire the skill to do, if we are members of a committed community. Members of such communities typically find exemplars, people whose lives and deaths embody the community virtues. They lift up those stories, tell them to one another, store them in the treasure-house of memory. And then, often in small ways, but sometimes in great ones, too, they live those stories out anew.

Now the interesting thing is that this present community has such an exemplary figure in its own past (and not only in its past). His name is Jesus, Jesus of Nazareth. We are about to engage in a ritual memory, an anamnesis, of *his* act of love of enemy. It seems we have the necessary exemplar, provided we want to follow him. Do we?

PART THREE

Looking Forward Again

(Nine Sermons)

Getting Started with God

In early autumn, one of the few youths in the church approached me and asked about becoming a church member. He was already active in the life of the church, and for him the transition to baptized membership would be an easy one. I talked with him about the conditions for this forward step, and arranged the further preparation he would need to take his full-fledged place among us.

The service arranged for his baptism would be one of the few in which we would honor all the remembering signs—baptism, prophetic preaching, and Lord's supper in one service. Our candidate, dressed in his baptismal white, would meet us at the appointed hour, and walking between the adult members who served as his mentors, he would march with me, similarly dressed, in procession behind the choir as it came singing down the center aisle of our meetingroom. I would lead all the congregation in the questions and responses that would position us before God as celebrants, and next the candidate and I would move down the steps into the waiting, open baptistry. There we would recite again the ancient words of baptism, and he would go under and emerge from the water, a new-washed child of God. After the sermon, he would join us at the Lord's table for his first share of its heavenly food. After the benediction, he would be led with his family into the fellowship hall to eat the cake and punch prepared for the occasion.

Knowing that all this would happen, what should I preach? It was not a time for a long sermon, and certainly not a time for massive theological reflection. Our candidate was youthful; why not, then, a Bible story of youth answering God? I selected the Samuel story, hoping that it would remain in memory as a guide to God whose self-giving shows the way for our own.

The boy Samuel was in the LORD's service under Eli. In those days the word of the LORD was rarely heard, and there was no outpouring of vision. One night Eli, whose eyes were dim and his sight failing, was lying down in his usual place, while Samuel slept in the temple of the LORD where the Ark of God was. Before the lamp of God had gone out, the LORD called him, and Samuel answered, "Here I am," and ran to Eli saying, "You called me; here I am." . . .

Then Eli understood that it was the LORD calling the boy; he told Samuel to go and lie down and said, "If someone calls once more, say, 'Speak, LORD; your servant is listening.'" So Samuel went and lay down in his place.

Then the LORD came, and standing there called, "Samuel, Samuel!" as before. Samuel answered, "Speak, your servant is listening."   (1 Sam. 3:1–5a, 8b–10)

[Also read Acts 9:17–19 and Luke 3:21f.]

Getting started with God may not come when we expect it. How old was Samuel when he heard the voice of God calling to him? We do not know, but the story in 1 Samuel 3 suggests that he was in latency, a time when a boy was old enough to have duties of his own and to keep night watch in the temple, and yet young enough to seek and trustingly accept the advice of Eli, an older man who was like a father to him. We may estimate that Samuel was eleven. To others, this decisive time of getting started with God comes sooner or it comes later, in young adulthood, or even (though this is rare) in old age. One famous conversion was that of Dag Hammarskjöld, who was forty-seven when he experienced the decisive turn that marked his entry into new life and prepared him for his service as United Nations Secretary General. So this getting-started sermon is not merely for or about youth, yet the boy Samuel is its central figure. From him we may learn what is needed to get started with God.

For that is what baptism, which together we have administered here today, is about. Every great human undertaking has its initiation ceremony, its act of inauguration. The practice of law starts with being admitted to the bar; marriage requires a wedding; fly-fishing really begins when you hook and play and land your first fish. Each of these adventures, great and small, has a time of preparation, and so it is with our journey with God. Our candidate today was preparing intensely for some time (you can ask him about it) with one of the members of this church assigned as his special preparation teacher, and he came to the baptismal waters well prepared. But this is not a sermon about the one who is baptized today; it is about the very idea, the biblical idea, of getting started with God.

I want to show you the elements of getting started, and invite you to apply them to your own life.

First, then, the story of Samuel, which you should read for yourself in 1 Samuel 3. You may recall that at the time of the story, Samuel was not living with his parents. His mother had long prayed for a child and had promised to dedicate that child to God. So when the prayer was answered, and the baby born and eventually weaned, she kept her promise, and gave little Samuel over to be a servant to Eli, the priest in the temple at Shiloh. In giving up the child, Hannah was returning to God the great gift she had been given. That may strike us as a strange, even fantastic or inhuman thing to do, but she was old and poor, and the prospect of a foster parent and a good life for her baby seemed neither cruel nor thoughtless: to Hannah and Elkanah the parents, it was the fulfillment of their high hopes and prayers.

Now see the other side of the story. You may think that growing up in the temple would have made it very easy for Samuel to hear the voice of God. How little you know! Who has not heard the story of the preacher's son who is a drunken rascal, the preacher's daughter who is flamboyantly naughty? Perhaps growing up behind the scenes, seeing the dirty linen of religious service, has insulated these young people from the good that is in their parents' lives. Or perhaps their parents' lives seen up close are not so good! This last, anyway, was Samuel's case, for Eli was a corrupt priest whom God had spurned, and his own sons were a bad example, as the boy Samuel could see daily. In his case, then, not much was to be expected. His parents had done a good thing, but it looked as if it were going to have only bad consequences. Though Samuel served in God's own temple, the God of the temple seemed far away indeed.

Then came Samuel's great night. Sleeping in the temple where the lamp of God burned before the ark, Samuel heard a voice calling him. Faithful fellow that he was, the boy went to his earthly master, old Eli. But Eli had not called! Back to bed, and the scene is repeated. Someone is calling, but it is not Eli. It happens a third time. And now something very lovely happens that need not have been a part of the story. How easy for Eli simply to say, "Go to bed and sleep, you little brat; don't wake me again." But Eli's priestly gifts are not completely lost. He senses what is happening. (If you and I are not what we should be, may we at least have enough of the grace of God to be sensitive to those around us, so that we may encourage what is happening in their lives.) Eli says, if you hear the voice again, know that God is calling, not I. Say, "Speak, LORD, your servant is listening" [3:9]. So Samuel lay down in his place, and the voice called, "Samuel, Samuel," as before [3:10]. And Samuel answered, "Speak; your servant is listening." And that was how he made his start with God.

What God then told Samuel seems just the right thing to say to a preadolescent—words of blame and judgment (and preteens flourish on some of that), but also words of promise about good days ahead—all well suited to the moral formation of a youth who has still to find his way. Today, though, there will not be time to tell you the rest of that story, for I must focus on the three things that helped Samuel get started with God.

First, Samuel was wise enough to seek out authority and experience. Uncertain what was happening that night, he went to the one he most trusted to help him understand what was going on. Old Eli the priest was frail and flawed, but he did know the tradition, and (bless him) he had the wit to realize what was happening to Samuel.

No one travels the biblical road alone; no one is so lonely, so devoid of help, but that you can turn to an older, wiser friend to ask for help. And one of the great duties of our church is to be sensitive and helpful when we see others starting the journey toward God.

Second, Samuel had an inner willingness to respond to the holy when it appeared to him. Never a rebel, he was ready for this great first step in his journey. When Eli told him how to answer the voice that called, "Samuel, Samuel," Samuel didn't scoff or ridicule or shy away in fear. This was something new; it was something momentous, and that night, I think, that boy became a man. He listened again for the voice. How does the hymn put it?

> *Have Thine own way, Lord, Have Thine own way.*
> *Thou art the potter, I am the clay;*
> *Mold me and make me After Thy will,*
> *While I am waiting, Yielded and still.*
> {*Adelaide Potter*}

When I, a perhaps precocious boy of ten or eleven, went to talk with my own pastor about becoming a Christian, he asked me if I would be willing to go away into the far mission field, to Africa, even, if God should call me. Quite truthfully, I was ready that minute, and said so. It occurred to me at the time that my pastor did not know how to set a hard test for a boy!

Third, Samuel took the right step to begin. In his case, that was quite simple. There was no baptism in those days. Eli told him to say these words, "Speak, LORD, for your servant is listening." And Samuel said it, and the God-journey began.

Sometimes people emphasize that we are saved by faith. I don't disagree with that, but it may be sadly misunderstood, for in the Bible, faith is not passive, it is active. The kind of faith that saves is active faith. When the Jesus movement began, there was already the practice that outsiders had to be baptized in order to become insiders (it was called "proselyte baptism"). What Jesus (and John the Baptist before him) made plain, though, is that as far as God is concerned, *all* of us begin as outsiders. Romans 3:23: "For all alike have sinned, and are deprived of the divine glory." That includes you and me, though we were born in Christian homes. That includes the children of the preacher and the deacon just as much as the children of the agnostic or the atheist. We are in the same fix, we have the same need, we belong to the same blood-bought band that Jesus has redeemed, and we like all the rest must make a start on the homeward journey if we are to be saved. As the Ethiopian said to Philip the evangelist long ago, "Look, here is water: what is to prevent my being baptized?" [Acts 8:36].

We Christians have another rite as well. It cannot take the place of the get-started rite; its purpose is quite different. For after we begin, we have to keep going, and the same grace of God that starts us off is available along the way, to keep us on that road. This food and drink for the journey, this remembering meal, this eucharist, is our way of saying thanks to God for mercies past, and it is God's way of reaching out to us to guide us along the way ahead. Again and again we come to this table, again and again we recall at this table the long journey past, and pledge anew to journey with the Master on the road ahead.

> *This is the hour of banquet and of song;*
> *This is the heavenly table spread for me;*
> *Here let me feast, and feasting, still prolong*
> *The brief, bright hour of fellowship with thee.*
>   *{Horatius Bonar}*

Christ Present: A Christmas Sermon

A church in trouble must employ gospel means to recover; once again there must be the glad flow of the good tidings from church to world. Many of our neighbors who had no regular church home would be looking about at Christmastime to celebrate what was for them only a seasonal observance—Santa Claus music, colored lights, family commotions and small joys. Actually, this winter celebration was never uniquely Christian; among the Mediterranean peoples it had been present as the seasonal celebration of the winter solstice, marked by the burning of fires and the exchange of gifts, long before Christian faith appeared.

Yet it made great good sense, now as then, for the church to take advantage of the cultural urge to celebration. We could conduct services that rang with the joy and glory of Christ's coming. The difficulty lay in doing this without permitting the actual good news to be swallowed up by the rhythms and practices of the folk religion. For the sentimental manger scenes in place on California lawns bore few clues as to the gospel itself.

Happily, January 2 was both the second Sunday of Christmas and the first Sunday of the month and thus our regular eucharist Sunday. This meant our service could be beautiful, simple, filled with Christmas music and climaxed by the great gospel sign of the broken body and shed blood. My sermonic task was to provide the conceptual and emotional bridge that would lead us from seasonal lights to the Light of the world. This sermon was my attempt.

To all who did accept him, to those who put their trust in him, he gave the right to become children of God, born not of human stock, by the physical desire of a human father, but of God. So the Word became flesh; he made his home among us, and we saw his glory, such glory as befits the Father's only Son, full of grace and truth.

John bore witness to him and proclaimed: "This is the man of whom I said, 'He comes after me, but ranks ahead of me,' before I was born, he already was."

From his full store we have all received grace upon grace; for the law was given through Moses, but grace and truth came through Jesus Christ. No one has ever seen God; God's only Son, he who is nearest to the Father's heart, has made him known.

(John 1:12–18)

Some people come to the end of Christmas curiously dissatisfied. Oh, they enjoyed it after a fashion. They liked the glitter and the lights—joy on little faces, love in courting couples' eyes, evident delight in hungry mouths at Christmas tables. Those were good moments. Still, the season did not quite fulfill its promise, did not bring the vaunted joy. Perhaps there were even tokens of inner peace: the singing of a carol, the memory of a mother's pain, a father's dread, a baby born, a shepherd's fright, an angel's song. These things convey to some a wonder and watchfulness, signalling again for us the deep hunger of human being as it reaches for God. And yet these are only hints, easily missed, and the dissatisfaction persists. Many are *sad* at Christmas, though they do not know why.

Perhaps, then, it is the gifts? How hard it is to give rightly: not too much (that is extravagance), not too little (that is stinginess). And if it is bad to be a bad giver, it is even worse to be a bad receiver. Yet how hard it is, when we hoped for *this,* to show proper gratitude for *that.* Perhaps gifts are never perfect—too much or too little, wrong size or wrong color, wrong gift or wrong giver! If that is so, is it because our expectations were too high? Because we wanted everything to be flawless? Because we wanted *the perfect gift?* For why should we, who are ourselves imperfect, and naturally so, even imagine there could be perfection?

Yet that is exactly what Christmas, the real Christmas, is about.

Not the tinsel and glitter, not the gatherings and the gifts, but *the* gift, the perfect gift that makes all giving graceful: Christ present, Christ who is God's presence, *Christ, God's present.* Let me show you that gift if I can, for until it is unwrapped, your Christmas has not fully come.

Did you notice that the beginning of John's Gospel tells about the great gift without a shred of the stories of manger and shepherds and angels? Nothing about oxen or asses or sheep or hay; nothing about wise men or stars or murderous kings. Nevertheless, here in John is the real truth, the only thing that must be believed, the central point of Christian Christmas. John 1:14 says,

> So the Word became flesh; he made his home among us, and we saw his glory, such glory as befits the Father's only Son, full of grace and truth.

Therefore, if Christmas depresses you or makes you sad, you have a perfect right, as a Christian, to set aside all these secondary Christmas tales and marginal Christmas practices—pack them up like so many tree ornaments, put them away—and with John's Gospel come straight to the point, the gift itself. "So the Word became flesh; he made his home among us."

How is that good news? What difference does it make?

For one thing, the original Christmas gift announces that *God enters fully into human life.* How do we think of God? As a remote First Cause, distant in the heavens, setting the cosmos upon its course? As the Shepherd of the stars? As the convergent point of eternity's energy? These are not wrong, but they are partial and therefore inadequate. Or do we think of God as a pervasive flux, a life within all life, everywhere present, nowhere evident, the evanescent soul of the world? Again not wrong, but again inadequate, and therefore by itself false.

For the good news is that God can be known as a man knows his brother or as a woman knows her sister. God is not only utterly other than we; God is not only within the world as beauty is within the rose. These things are so, but it is also true that "the Word became flesh; he made his home among us." Can you talk to God? Ask if his friends could talk to Jesus. Can you follow God? Ask if the disciples could follow Jesus. Can you suffer for God, serve God, be loyal to God? Yes, yes, yes, for "the Word became flesh; he made his home among us." Here is the real point of Christmas: God comes to be with us; God can therefore be *known.*

From this, says John's Gospel, it follows that *our human birthright can be reclaimed.* It is a great thing to have a birthright. Last week I was with my wife's parents at their ranch in western Nebraska's sand hills. The Murphy family is consciously Irish. On the ranch house wall hangs a memento of a family trip to distant Ireland. This is a certificate from the "Ancestral Land Company of Ireland" certifying that one Richard Murphy of Nebraska has under lease one square foot of County Sligo. Symbolically, one Murphy has reclaimed his birthright. If he can only keep his feet close together, he has a place to stand on the old sod.

Yet the entire human race (including even the Irish) has a different birthright. Genesis declares that we are made "in the image of God" [1:27]. In other words, we are made to be godlike, each of us. Only by our sin could we have lost that birthright; yet lose it we have. Then Jesus came, and showed the way, not to Ireland, but to the kingdom of God, where our birthright awaits us now, a birthright many sections long and wide that we can recover not because of our race, or ancestry, or our achievements, but courtesy of Jesus who was born on Christmas Day. As John 1:12 says,

> To all who did accept him, to those who put their trust in him,
> he *gave the right* to become children of God.

Hence the age-old estrangement of God's people is ended. Hence the meaning of Christmas rings clear: If I will receive the Word who became flesh, God's family can include even me.

That God can be known, that our human birthright, our square mile in the kingdom of heaven, is reclaimed—these are elements of the Christmas gospel, "the Word became flesh; he made his home among us." Yet there is in our text still a third element: *there is a people, a family, of God,* whose role it is even now *to embody Christ's ongoing presence in the world.* Verse 16 says it clearly:

From his full store we have all received grace upon grace.

This "we all" is the people of God, sharers in faith, you and I, if we believe.

Think for a moment how reasonable, how natural, this aspect of the gift really is. Suppose God had originally intended to win back the world by self-investment, taking up a unique human life. Suppose that human life that would restore us to God was not to be lived in one of the nations we call great: Jesus was not to be a Persian, or an Egyptian, or a Roman. Jesus was not to be an Irishman, or a German, or a Frenchman, or even a Scot. Jesus did not appear as a Japanese, or a Russian, or (thank heaven!) as an American. Jesus was a Jew—one of God's own people, yet a people small, out of the way, despised by many. This presented a problem, though. In that case, how could Jesus' way become known to Persians or French or Russians or Americans? Become known, not just by a story, but—as it was in Palestine—by firsthand contact? How could the Americans ever grasp the gospel? It could only happen if the risen Christ were to come to America and visit us here. Only if once again "the Word became flesh; he made his home among *us.*" Only if there is now a people called Immanuel, a people for all peoples, a people who are learning to live by grace because grace *has* come to their neighborhood.

The old Latin hymn "O Come, All Ye Faithful" is partly about a pilgrim people marching to Bethlehem to see what has come to pass: *Venite, venite, in Bethlehem* (Come ye, O come ye to Bethlehem). But that pilgrim procession of which we sing, the adoration of the child in the manger, is possible only because of a more profound "coming." The English version, you may remember, starts out, "O come, all ye faithful." And this time, the Latin word for "come" is not *venite* but *adeste*—which simply means "be present." All our pilgrimages, all our Christmas parades, all our solemn worship is empty unless by benefit of that original presence of his; our presence with God depends upon God's prior presence with us. "So the Word became flesh; he made his home among us, and we saw his glory." By that holy presence, we are presented, present-ed, to the Holy One and so to one another as his kin.

Then the good news of Christmas, the core good news (not the tinsel and the lights, not even the shepherds and the angels, but the heart of the matter) is this: "So the Word became flesh." Which, as we have seen, is to say:

> We can know God, for God knows us.

> We can reclaim humanity's birthright.

> We are assigned the role of a witness people, living the life that Jesus brought to all life.

That is the Christ present; that is the good news to all.

Part of Christmas satisfaction is good eating. After the fasting and waiting of Advent comes the celebration, Jesus' twelve-day birthday party. What a time! Yet it does not always satisfy. At one meal, I ate too much. Was I satisfied? No, I was miserable. At another meal, trying to compensate, I ate too little, and again was uncomfortable. It's almost like Christmas gifts, isn't it—too many or too few, too great or too small, and we are not satisfied. Yet there is a meal, a feast, ordained by Jesus in the days of his flesh: "Do this in memory of me" [1 Cor. 11:24]. When we share this meal, the tiniest bite and least sip will satisfy, for they are the sign, the evidence, of the presence of the Lord, and in truth it is with him that we share, on him that we feed, by his presence that we are filled. He is the true Christmas present, the true feast. Come then, and renew your baptismal pledge at this table; come to the real Christmas feast.

SERMON 20

Fishing for Friends

Our church's biggest visible need was membership growth that did not depend merely upon enlisting our children (of whom there were not many) or upon receiving new arrivals from other parts of the country (once again, not many). Instead, we needed to evangelize, and that meant reaching out to potential Christians who did not yet realize that God was calling them into the fellowship of our church.

A natural pool from which such newcomers might be drawn was the circle of acquaintances and friends of present members. We had tried various schemes to encourage folk to bring their unchurched friends along to our events with them. These efforts produced little or nothing, and I puzzled over the reason. Gradually it sank in upon me: Our members for the most part had no friends other than one another and a few members of other churches. They lived in a small world of congenial fellow Christians.

In this, of course, they were not exceptional. We dwelt in a vast metropolitan region—second largest in the United States—that consisted in people alongside one another rather than people with one another. Privacy was the first rule of our region's social structure. People coped with the throb and throng of megalopolis by keeping strictly to their own circles—their own families, their own ethnic groups, their own church members. Ours functioned simply as one more such small group.

Yet this invisible isolation was one the gospel was set to overcome. How was it to do so here? How were we to scale the walls that shut us off from others who (if they only knew it) were thirsting for the water of life?

The answer was plain: before there could be evangelism, there must be pre-evangelism. Before anyone new could hear the good news, we had to pave avenues of trust along which the good news could travel. I hit upon the Johannine metaphor of friendship: the church must

141

become friends to many if Jesus was to be their saving friend. My text, though, came not from John's Gospel, but from the Gospel of Luke and the familiar story of recruiting "fishers of people." Yet I confronted in my flock a distaste for what they saw evangelism to be: I would have to describe this preevangelistic task in a way that made it seem credible, possible, to our people, who were quite literally afraid of the task that now lay before us. In that case, it was important that I maintain good cheer right to the end. (The reader can see whether or not I did so.)

> When Simon saw what had happened he fell at Jesus's knees and said, "Go, Lord, leave me, sinner that I am!" For he and all his companions were amazed at the catch they had made; so too were his partners James and John, Zebedee's sons. "Do not be afraid," said Jesus to Simon; "from now on you will be catching people."   (Luke 5:8–10)

"Don't be afraid. From now on, you will be catching people." But of course, that was just what Simon the fisherman *was* afraid of. Simon was comfortable enough as owner and operator of a fishing fleet. He knew that line of work. You had your customers. You worked by night. You had your boats; you had your employees; you had your lake. It was hard work, but you knew how to do it.

Now, everything was changing. Simon had met Jesus. They were in different lines of work. Simon fished. Jesus was—well, what *did* Jesus do? He was not exactly a rabbi, and not exactly a physician, and not exactly a political revolutionary, though there was something of all these in him.

One thing couldn't be dismissed: Jesus was by now clearly Simon's friend. When one of Simon's family members had been desperately ill, Jesus had visited, done his spell or exorcism or whatever it was he did, and the sick one got well. And Simon was Jesus' friend, too: if Jesus wanted to go fishing in broad daylight after a night's work, Simon his friend would provide the boat and the nets—and Jesus did have the most unbelievable luck! So they were friends. Only now, Jesus was making some very difficult demands: Quit your job! Leave the business! Come with me! You are going to catch people from now on. It was scary. Well might Jesus say, "Don't be afraid"! Simon *was* afraid.

And so will you be, perhaps. That is, you will be afraid when you hear what I am going to say to you. For I tell you that this word from Jesus, "Don't worry, from now on you will be catching people," from this day on applies to this congregation. We are about to go fishing. And that's scary, exactly because we don't know what it means. Let's see if we can get it in focus.

First, some things that it does not mean. It does not mean that we are going to be buttonholing strangers, cornering them, telling them they are doomed and damned if they don't listen to our religious ideas. Heaven forbid! I would expect that the worst thing I could possibly do for the kingdom of God is to start trying to push my religious ideas upon strangers. In the first place, they will not hear what I say; they will only hear that Christians are a pushy, unpleasant bunch, rather like the fake beggars in airports, people you'd rather avoid. Duck, dodge, here comes a Christian! But "fishing for people" doesn't mean anything like that.

Second, it doesn't mean that you have memorized a little formula for making Christians, which you will toss off to strangers or acquaintances. Step one. Step two. Step three, you're saved. My experience with becoming a Christian was not like that; I believe yours was not, either. I think the only people surely helped by such formulas are the ones who produce them. Formulas may clarify Christian teaching in their minds (and that is good), but they are not likely to clarify matters for real outsiders.

Then what does it mean, this strange prediction made by Jesus? Catching people? Let me remind you of a Wednesday evening last summer when we met in the social hall, at the end of the course led by our teachers. We talked for close to an hour then about how our own journeys with Jesus had begun. Some had difficulty putting a finger on the beginning time. Others spoke of church summer camp, and how what really mattered to them today had become dominant in their thoughts and feelings then. Someone spoke of "times when it seemed God was touching me." Someone else spoke of her baptism: "It was a big awakening for me"—a wet awakening, that one! Someone else spoke of being led along by providential signs—things worked out in such a way as to say, "For you, this is the way." More than one of you spoke of making a beginning, and then drifting away, only to be summoned back, somehow, and realizing that (and once again, I quote), "I had experienced failure and was myself a sinner." One of our teachers told a story as dramatic as himself, and the other (who happens to be my wife) told one as low-keyed yet compelling as her lovely self.

These stories all had one earmark of truth that a teacher is trained to notice: each story was so different from the others that they could hardly have been copied. What did they have in common? Well, there was this: People who come to Jesus seem to do so while they are in touch with Jesus' other people. Whether it was summer camp, or Christian family, or the regular, ongoing life of the church, Christian community provided a context in which new Christians found their place. Even in that setting, it didn't happen to all: many told of brothers or sisters in the same family who had the same context but missed out and drifted away. Yet for those who followed Jesus, this being around other Christians was essential. The stories you told had some other things in common, too, but for now let us concentrate upon this role of community in helping each along the way.

Notice that the same thing is true in the story of the earliest Christians: they, too, began by being there with the others, and, of course, the magnet was Jesus himself. To one another, they were *friends*. Later, according to one Gospel, Jesus reminded them of that: "I have called you friends," he said [John 15:15]. Jesus was other things to them as well: he was their teacher; in time they would come to see the presence of God in him; ultimately they knew him as "Lord." In the beginning, though, he simply became their friend, and they his. Notice, too, that they did not seek him out; Jesus took the initiative. We do have some stories of people asking to follow Jesus, but not all who ask are accepted. He chose the ones he wanted; it was with them that he made friends. What Jesus was asking Simon to do, that day by the lake, was to start doing what Jesus himself had been doing—fishing for friends. Why did he call it that? Because Simon was in the fishing business. If Simon had been a metal caster, perhaps Jesus would have said, "From now on, you are going to mold people, not iron or brass." And if Simon had been a schoolteacher, maybe Jesus would have said, "From now on, you are going to teach school, not for children, but for grown-ups." Since Simon fished, Jesus said, "Let's go fishing for people." It was what Jesus did, turned into language Simon could understand.

Now that is in line with what Jesus is saying to us. As Jesus has been a friend to you, it's time for you to be a friend to others. How will this work?

There are some special things about friendship that distinguish it from other sorts of human relations. First, friends are not family. Your family has a special claim upon you that no one else does—and you have a special claim upon them. Yet the wonder of friendship is that you don't have to be blood kin to your friends. It may be better if you aren't. Friends can be very different from *everybody* in your family, and still be friends with you. They are, if you will let me say it, a certain relief, compared to family with its long memories and old ties and (not seldom) old grudges. With a friend, you start off with a clean slate. Also, friends are not lovers. Maybe sex makes the world turn, as the soap operas teach, but it is not very likely that friends will become lovers, and lovers rarely become friends unless they get married first.

What is it, then, that makes a friend? First of all, it is helping one another. You are trying to move a big rock in your garden; it is really too heavy for you. Someone sees you, stops, and helps. It is a friendly act. C. S. Lewis (in a book called *The Four Loves*) says that friends are always friends *about* something—they collect stamps together, or they repair cars, or they cook, or they talk politics. Or like Simon and Jesus, they fish! Find someone you can do things with: if you do, you are about to find a friend.

The next stage in friendship is trusting. We can trust people too soon with too much, creating a burden the friend cannot bear. Then disappointment follows, one or the other feels betrayed, the friendship fails. The other mistake, though (and I think this one is my own) is trusting too little, living too much within ourselves, not risking anything by letting ourselves fall into the others' hands. Friends do take risks, and successful risking makes a friendship grow.

So there are two steps in friendship. One is reaching out in friendly ways to the people you encounter. That was what Jesus had been doing when he got acquainted with the men on the lake—making friends. It doesn't seem a bad thing for anyone. But it is a special duty for followers of Jesus.

The other step must come at the right time, but come it must. It is a step that involves the risk of trusting your friend. This is the move that twelve-step people make when for the first time they stand up in a meeting and say, "My name is Mary, and I am an alcoholic." It's frightening. What if the other scorns your self-disclosure? What if your friend doesn't want to hear that you are a sinner, saved by grace? What if the fragile friendship you have now can't stand that truth? Yet to have a friend, you must offer him or her yourself, bit by bit, and not merely a prettified self-portrait. You are a Christian. Admit it! You must sooner or later admit to your would-be friends that you already have another friend, a friend called Jesus.

I can't tell you how to take this second step. I recognize that I am not very good at it myself. I tend to protect myself with silence, concealment. But without this second step—without letting your flawed, real self show—how can you possibly hope that the other will show himself or herself to you? And if he or she won't, your acquaintance is doomed to stay in the shallows, never launching out into the deep with Jesus [Luke 5:4].

❖ ❖ ❖

Where does all this leave us? Jesus is a friend to Simon and James and John. He says to them, "Don't be afraid; from now on, you will be catching people." He means that just as he has fished for their friendship, and gained it, now they, too, must fish for friends. They must give others the chance to become what they have become. They were afraid to do this—that's why he said, "Don't be afraid."

Now let me for a moment be your teacher. As one who believes in homework, I want to give you two assignments. The first is this: Start clearing a path for a new friendship. Maybe that will lead to something more, maybe not. For now, that doesn't matter. But the assignment is clear: You are to act as a friend would toward somebody not now your friend. Go next door; go across to the next work station at your office; pay attention to somebody in the market where you shop. Don't hand him or her a tract; don't invite him or her to church; don't give him or her advice. Save all that now—or save it forever. But for somebody, this week, just be friendly. It is assignment number one.

Assignment number two may be harder. Practically everyone here already has some friends outside this church. They are co-workers, neighbors, sports fans, members of your ride group, members of your club. This week, risk letting one of those existing friends see inside your life. If that means admitting you follow Jesus, admit it. If it means admitting you have a drinking problem, admit that, too. If it means admitting you are an extremely shy person, say so! Let your guard down a little, for it will open the way to trust.

I realize that both these assignments are difficult for some of you. So like any good teacher, I am going to give you a way to make it easier. Here it is: Jesus is already your friend—the one you can really trust. Talk to Jesus this week about the trouble my homework makes for you. If Jesus won't help, phone me up (you've got my number), and we'll figure out why, together. I'd like to be your friend, too.

SERMON 21

Springtime in the Kingdom of God

In the short run, at least, the changes I had urged in the previous sermon did not take place—not in any way I could observe. To say the least, no one phoned me to find out why Jesus wasn't helping with the homework! Nevertheless, I felt it important to keep pressing for change. It was too easy for us to slip back into the old, comfortable ways, easy to do what we had done for forty years or more, easy to neglect the challenges of word and witness and worship that confronted the church and that must be met if we were to survive. (And in the long run, some of the needed changes in our congregation did occur.)

Yet preaching could not be all pressure. Lent was at hand; it was not the custom of our folk to "give up" something for Lent or to take on fresh spiritual disciplines. We were content to make this traditional season simply an item on the church bulletin for a few weeks. I hoped to make it something more, and yet I did not mean to add to the existing pressure. Perhaps I could seize on the old theme of Christian liberty in a fresh way?

Here I was much helped by a commentary on Mark's Gospel, Binding the Strong Man, *written by a friend and former student of mine, Ched Myers. His reading of Mark emphasized the revolutionary nature of the good news, and I tried to match some of its insights in ways that would capture the imagination of my own hearers.*

There was risk here, however. If I emphasized the strictures from which Jesus liberated his (Jewish) followers, would I not seem to endorse the old Christian slander of today's Jews as people living under harsh law (while we Christians, of course, lived by a free gospel)? I tried to avoid this by reminding my listeners, toward the end of the sermon, how easily our own way of life became constrictive not liberative.

It was at this time that Jesus came from Nazareth in Galilee and was baptized in the Jordan by John. As he was coming up out of

149

the water, he saw the heavens break open and the Spirit descend on him like a dove. And a voice came from heaven: "You are my beloved Son; in you I take delight."

At once the Spirit drove him out into the wilderness, and there he remained for forty days tempted by Satan. He was among the wild beasts; and angels attended to his needs.

After John had been arrested, Jesus came into Galilee proclaiming the gospel of God: "The time has arrived; the kingdom of God is upon you. Repent, and believe the gospel."

(Mark 1:9–15)

The days are now getting longer. Although our cool Southern California weather still prevails, winter's brief reign here is ended. Spring has come. Soon migratory birds will tell us what already the pansies and daffodils are saying—it is springtime! You notice in the church bulletin that this is the first Sunday in *Lent,* an English word akin to "lengthen," referring to the longer days of spring. Lent itself simply means spring: a time for spring cleaning, a time for new beginnings, a time to throw off the wintry burden of dark days and ill thoughts and old fears and welcome God's renewal of the earth. Even in the most ancient times, Christians sensed a connection between the changing weather and the good news that the church lives by. This can be for us not a sad time or a *Fastenzeit* (fast time) in the church's life, but a glad time.

Who wouldn't be glad about spring? Spring fever is our name for that slightly lazy, footloose feeling that comes over us when the days grow warmer. How nice it would be, we think, to break away from all the endless duties, maybe get in the car, drive somewhere else, do something else. For years I had a convertible—not good for freeways, but great for country roads. What could be sweeter than the spring air rushing through that car, supposing a delightful companion next to me, and the smells and sounds of the countryside everywhere. This is not mere whimsy: We are made for change, and the change in the weather cries out for a change in ourselves. Springtime is change time.

We have been following the life story of Jesus, but we have gotten ahead of ourselves. Long before the ecstasy and agony of being with Jesus on the mountaintop, even before Jesus invited his friends to go with him fishing for friends, there was a springtime in Jesus' life, a beginning time. We could call it springtime in the kingdom of God.

A strange character had come into the country where Jesus lived, a man named John. John preached repentance—a new start—and dipped people in Jordan's waters, baptized them, to signify that if now they awaited what God would do next, for them life was starting over. Jesus, who had been brought up in a good home, Jesus who was serious and meant to do whatever God wanted, Jesus who recognized in himself unusual gifts, an unusual destiny—Jesus went out with the others to hear this John preach.

Now to understand what happened next, you have to know something about Palestine, the little land where Jesus, along with many other Jews, made his home. First, it was a very old land. Off and on for two thousand years the Jews had lived there, beginning with their mysterious ancestor Abraham, a man for whom God had also had a mission. In Jesus' day this people had little enough in the way of wealth or power, but they kept in their care extremely old books, going back to the time of Moses' stone tables of the law. Alongside these ancient books were many customs, some of them very old as well—what could be eaten and couldn't be eaten, what could be touched and must not be touched, what was pure and what was impure. You could spend your whole life just learning those rules. A class of people called scribes, religious lawyers, so to speak, did nothing else.

By themselves, those circumstances might have made for a complicated but lovely life, but in addition to the purity rules just mentioned there was another set of rules, laid down by the existing laws of debt and inheritance and tax. Palestine was occupied by Rome (as it had previously been occupied by Parthia, by Persia, by Egypt, by Macedonia, by Babylon). There were the local rulers, so-called kings, such as Herod, who were not kings in the line of David at all, but mere puppets fawning for the favor of their Roman masters. Layered over these local kings was Rome, itself a vast empire something like the Soviet Union of a few years ago, a military dictatorship with harsh economic laws to drain the wealth of the provinces. In the name of all these masters there came the tithe collectors, the rent collectors, the tax collectors, the local debt collectors. People were trapped by debt. No expert myself, I added up all that a Palestinian farmer was supposed to pay; it came to 110 percent of anyone's income. So a plain worker couldn't simply keep the law— couldn't afford to; and he couldn't stay out of debt—the debt laws would get you. There was no way out.

Jesus, watching the long line of "sinners" waiting to be baptized by John in the river Jordan, knew all that. Indeed, those same laws, the debt code and the purity code, encircled him as much as anyone else. Meanwhile, John stood preaching God's kingdom coming. Jesus made up his mind. This springtime, he himself would break free of the social prison of custom. He took his place in the line of men and women waiting to be baptized. Into the water went Jesus. Out of the water he came, "free at last," God's Spirit descending to provide for his need, God's voice proclaiming, "You are my beloved Son; in you I take delight" [Mark 1:11]. It was indeed springtime, beginning time, in the realm of the Rule of God.

How do we know that Jesus was a break-free human being? How do we know that getting free was his theme? Because in all the rest of Mark's Gospel, and in every Gospel, the life that he led and summoned others to lead was such a free life. He was not stopped by sickness, and there was plenty of sickness then. He confronted paralyzed people, and when they met him they were freed up. He met "sinners," people locked into their sins, and he exempted them. Read the opening chapters of Mark: there, when Jesus comes, folk are set free.

Yes, it is true that finally the system caught up with Jesus, true that he did not escape it. He went to Jerusalem; arrested, he carried a Roman cross to his own place of execution; he suffered; he died. All that did happen. Yet when it comes time in a few weeks for us to recall those crucial events here, we will see that *even then* Jesus in a strange way remained free; it was almost as if he were the ruler, and the Sanhedrin and Pontius Pilate and the soldiers were the slaves, doing what they did in helpless bondage to the system Jesus had rejected. And finally it was God who decided who would be free from the tomb they had prepared. The freedom Jesus accepted at his baptism was the freedom God gives those who ask.

Now you may be asking, in all seriousness, what any of this has to do with us. We are not ancient Palestinians; we do not live by a purity code, by a debt code. We are Americans; we claim freedom as our birthright.

Don't be too sure, though. Are you indeed what God meant you to be? Or are you cornered by life's expectations—that keep you from fulfilling God's good plan for your life? I wonder if we older members even truly remember our youthful dreams, can even recall what we meant to be, what we then believed God meant us to be. Circumstances interfered, our country (as they say) called us, our families made demands, society laid its expectations upon us. What ever became of *our* springtime? And for you who are not so far along as the rest—is it really true that freedom's heady breezes now blow through your life? Are you really headed for the destiny God has for you? Or is it already true that social norms, others' expectations, what parents want, what the school demands, what your peers think fitting, all close the circle around you, so that you are not your own woman, not your own man?

I do not know, but let me tell you this true story. In a church I know not a thousand miles from here, there was a married couple. For her, it was a second marriage—her earlier marriage had failed, and although she had remained on friendly terms with her former spouse, life had taken a new course. Her new husband was devoted to her, and they were happily Christian together. Now came sad news. Her former husband was ill; indeed, he was dying of cancer. He had not remarried, and there were no other responsible family members.

Medical expenses were high. He needed a place to stay and be ill—literally, a place to die. So the former wife and new husband took him into their own home, gave him a room, and provided for him there as best they could.

So far, we seem to be hearing an authentic Jesus story. Here were people—unconventional, certainly—who were trying to let the love of Jesus take control of their home.

But I haven't told you the last part of the story. This couple came under severe criticism. That criticism came from within their own church. They were criticized for taking the dying spouse into their home. For they had committed a sin against the iron conventions of romantic American society. They had broken the valentine rule that said we must each progress from romance to romance to romance, never looking back. This disconcerting Christian couple had instead acted according to the free love of Jesus, disregarding the romantic conventions of their California suburb. They were made to feel ashamed in their own church!

There is a happy ending to this story. The pastor came to their rescue. In public he praised the hospitality they had offered; he shamed the shamers; he defended the freedom of Jesus' people to be like Jesus.

I cannot tell you that the matter will be so swiftly settled in every case, or that if you exercise your freedom in Jesus Christ the outcome will always be happy. Remember what happened to Jesus himself.

Today, though, it is springtime; today we have a right to the rites of spring. Today the topic is freedom.

Here is one worry. What if people get free, but then the new situation becomes oppressive, so that they become prisoners of the new just as once they were prisoners of the old? Concretely, can't church itself become a prison, keeping people from the rich, fulfilling lives that God promises them? The answer is, of course it can. From time to time in church history that has indeed happened. With good intentions, churches have made rules every bit as constricting as the purity code and the debt code that crushed the people in Jesus' day. What then? Why then God must send a prophet to cry liberty afresh. "Let my people go," said Moses to the Pharaoh, and "let my people go," God will say again to church structures whenever they confine and crush human life. Life must be free to fulfill what God intends. God always sends a prophet; you can be sure that it will happen again when needed. You can trust God.

A bigger worry about freedom's springtime is this: can I myself really turn loose? I'm old, says one, and I have so many obligations, so many people expect things of me, I'm so set in my habits, I'll never get free. Or another says, I'm in my middle years, and so many people count on me; how can I be free and still true to all these dependents? Or a youth says, I know myself; my will is weak. I can promise to turn loose and follow Jesus, but I don't think I can resist the pressure from my friends.

Let us be truthful here, too: it will be hard. But in the Jesus story, God's Spirit, the infinite power of God, was there to make liberty happen. Jesus was tempted; you will be tempted as well. Yet by the power of the Spirit of God, Jesus overcame, and you will, too. Here is a helpful note: even Jesus needed a sign from God. For him as for us, that sign was baptism. If you need the sign, the time is right, for we should be planning a baptism in our church very soon. God offers the signs; God comes to us as Spirit. The message is, "Break loose; it's springtime." How about you?

Did Sarah Laugh?

I set about to accomplish many things with this sermon (and attempting too much may have been its doom). Still strongly aware of our need for evangelism, I wanted to press some practical steps upon the church—one, forming a new adult Sunday school class that might enlist new congregants; another, generating a list of "friends of the church" that could be used to enlarge our mailings.

The lectionary we followed led me to the text in Isaiah, and that in turn to the story in Genesis that lay behind the Isaiah passage. It seemed possible to treat God's promise of a child to Sarah and Abraham in their old age as analog of a promise offered to our church: our "Isaacs" would be the newcomers God would add to our congregation in answer to our faith.

At the same time, though, the treatment of Sarah in the sermon responded to another felt need: enhancing the dignity and power of our own Sarahs, our own church women, who had for too long suffered in the church and in American culture due to their gender alone.

Each of these three goals, the enhancement of our evangelism, the promotion of projects associated with it, and the honoring of the church's women, was worthy, and each in a way grew from the texts I found before me. Yet in retrospect, I attempted too much. In the event, the projected list never materialized, and the class, though it did begin, was less than successful. Readers may judge for themselves how well the third sermon goal was met. The lesson I take from this is, make haste slowly.

> Sarah said, "God has given me good reason to laugh, and everyone who hears will laugh with me."　　　　　　(Gen. 21:6)

Consider the rock from which you were hewn,
the quarry from which you were cut;
consider Abraham your father
and Sarah who gave you birth
when I called him he was but one;
I blessed him and made him many.

(Isa. 51:1–2)

What is this mention of Sarah, the remote ancestor of the people of Israel, doing here in the book of Isaiah the prophet? Her story, such as it is, has been told long before, in the middle chapters of Genesis, in connection with the settlement of Israel's forebears, the so-called patriarchs, in the land of promise. There is no further discussion of Sarah in the rest of the Hebrew Bible. This is not likely to surprise us: we suppose that in the Old Testament it was male descent that mattered, and we do not expect to hear as much about women. No, the surprise is that in this key verse in Isaiah, Abraham and Sarah are given equal billing: he is "the rock from which you were hewn," but she, in precise poetic parallel, is "the quarry from which you were cut." Abraham heard God's call, but Sarah carried and then gave birth to Isaac, who in turn fathered a multitude in Israel. Perhaps we should know more than we do about this woman, for she shows up again in the Epistle to Hebrews as a prime example of faith [Heb. 11:1].

Yet in the earlier Genesis episode, this same Sarah is caught laughing at God! Certainly that was not a nice thing to do! Nevertheless it happened, and I had better tell you the story, so that you can judge from the evidence what she was actually like—and how like her we in this church may be.

"Beautiful adventurer" might have been the way her friends remembered Sarah. Her very name, "princess," suggests elegance and attractiveness; certainly Abraham the traveler was not blind to her charms. They were married in ancient Ur, cradle of culture, and together they moved west in search of a new home. It was no dust bowl migration, even when God sent them farther west still, to Canaan land. They moved, and with them went kinfolk, possessions, dependents, herds—all that rich ranchers might want in a new place. And Sarah, stunning Sarah, went west as well.

Her story takes more telling than we have time to tell. There were travel adventures, as this beautiful young married woman spent a season in an Egyptian harem. And there were household adventures, as Sarah struggled to maintain her place despite one tremendous Near Eastern handicap—she never did conceive a child. (For child meant heritage, a heritage that God had solemnly promised Abraham.) The years drifted by, and no child was born to continue the line of promise. Small wonder if Sarah's elegance was streaked with discontent. The very servants in the household mocked her childless state. She approached menopause, and then was past it, and it seemed the promise would not be kept.

Then on a fateful day, when the ranch headquarters tents were pitched in the oak grove at Mamre, there was a mysterious visit to Sarah's ranch—see Genesis 18. Even the number of the visitors shifts within this strange, numinous story: first Scripture reports "three men"; then "one of them" speaks; finally, the voice is not that of one man or three, but it is "the LORD" who speaks. The mystery of the visitor is compounded by the mystery of his motive. At first this seems to be a story about Near Eastern hospitality. There is much ado about the washing of feet, resting in the shade, and "a little food," which turns out to be a barbecue with homemade bread and fresh milk and curds and roast veal. Then the visit becomes an inquiry about Sarah—who had quite properly remained out of sight in the tent (too many men had already taken an improper interest in her), but these visitors seem to know her name, anyway. And at the climax of this story, the visitor (now one, not three) predicts, "Next year I will return and she will have a son." This is to be not only a pregnancy fathered by centenarian Abraham, wonder enough, but also a postmenopausal conception and birthing by Sarah. "Is anything too hard for the LORD?" [Gen. 18:14].

It was in any case too much for Sarah, and behind the tent flap, she giggled. The stranger hears. "Why did Sarah laugh?" he demands, and Sarah politely lies; "I didn't." Yet the visitor is not deceived: "You did laugh," he declares.

There is a glorious last chapter in this story. This aging beauty conceives; a child is born, his name already chosen; he is Isaac, which means laughter. The promise is kept; the line is preserved; God has not lied. Sarah the disappointed, Sarah the barren beauty, Sarah the scornful, becomes against all likelihood Sarah, mother of Isaac, Sarah, mother of future Israel. According to Genesis 21:6, on the day of his birth Sarah declared:

> God has given me good reason to laugh, and everyone who hears
> will laugh with me.

A scornful giggle has become the laughter of joy; the beautiful adventurer has gained her place in the world's future. Despite all the vagaries of nature and history, God the faithful has kept faith. When the prophet Isaiah, twelve centuries later, recalls Israel to faith, he will remind his readers of Abraham—but also of laughing Sarah. This princess is not only the great-grandmother of twelve tribes of Israel. She is also ancestor to all who have faith in a God for whom nothing is too hard, a God who turns giggles into guffaws, who turns doubt into faith, disbelief into rejoicing.

Do you see why Sarah is our ancestor, too? The original promise to Abraham was to have a great multitude of descendants:

> Look up at the sky, and count the stars, if you can. So many will
> your descendants be.   [Gen. 15:5]

How many stars are there? I don't know, and whatever I learned would be out of date shortly; new stars are found every year. The point is that Abraham could not count the stars, nor would he be able to count his descendants.

Moreover, the promise to Sarah went this way [Gen. 17:16]:

She will be the mother of nations.

Not of *a* nation (that would be wonderful), but of *nations.* How was this to happen? The New Testament answer is that faith would flow to disciples in all nations, faith through the risen Christ, in the mission of the Spirit of God. Christians are not made by the cradle but by the gospel; we do not enter God's kingdom by "human stock" [John 1:13], but by the Word who comes from God.

Let us take this church as a concrete example of that outflow of faith. Sarah was in her nineties when she learned she would become a mother. Though our congregation's beginning is somewhat obscure, I believe we like Sarah are now in our tenth decade as well. Like Sarah, we perhaps supposed at first that God would multiply our numbers by natural regeneration—Christian parents would have Christian children, world without end. It has not worked that way. So, like our ancient grandmother in the faith, we have to depend upon faith, the faith of new Christians whom God will provide so that our faith can live on. God has not stopped caring about the future. We may be tempted to hide behind the tent flap and snicker at God's promise, but it is risky indeed to laugh at God.

I thought I heard someone say, "Oh, we missed our chance; once we were a growing congregation, but now our time is passed. We are past the menopause." I thought I heard someone say, "How can God give children in faith to an aging congregation? That doesn't happen, does it?" I thought I heard some cynic say, "No matter if God's promise is not kept; whoever believed that, anyway?"

Banish all these sick unbeliefs. What I want to hear is the giggle of another Sarah behind the tent flap—a Sarah who says, "What a wonderful promise! Could it possibly apply to me?" Before we are done, I hope to hear the laughter of Sarah on the day of Isaac's birth—Isaac whose name means laughter, Isaac who is the child of God's promise. Before our time together is ended, I hope to hear laughter at the fulfillment of God's promise—a promise we brought to words last fall and posted in our church entryway.

Perhaps you say, "I don't see how it will happen." Well, we must learn to see. Let me give just two examples of faithful seeing.

We are about to compile a list of people who need the ministry of this church. Not our absent members—we have their names, and we care about them. No, new people, acquaintances and friends in this city, in this valley, whom we know. From that list, still more will develop. But first, the list. I ask you to provide names and addresses. No exact rule can be made, but suppose each man, woman, and youth who is a member here provides only four names of people who would benefit from this church. That should give us a list of nearly two hundred names as a start. You don't need to find out if they want to be on the list; we will find that out. They may be family; they may be neighbors; they may be friends at your club, coworkers at your job, clients in your business, folk who help you and whom you will honor by listing. Especially must we remember those distinguished but disadvantaged folk for whom this church provides an opportunity not otherwise available to them. When we have the list, I will show you the next step, but now, like Sarah of old recording unborn Isaac's name, we must make a list. We must have faith.

Second, we are now going to begin yet another adult class. This time one of our seminarians will be the new teacher. One or two members may be borrowed as seed from other classes, but most of the new class members will be people not yet regular in any class. As these classes grow, we shall grow, and this is the next important step along our way. For more information, see me after church. We'll start next week, with great literature and a fine teacher!

Back to the question: Did Sarah laugh? I'll say! More to the point, is our barren beauty of a church about to laugh? I hope so! I hope we laugh, with Sarah of old, and like her cry, "Everyone who hears will laugh with me," because what we are going to do is gloriously happy, fit for the Easter laughter of the children of God.

SERMON 23

The Thirteenth Cross

There was serious work to be done in our church, changes we needed to make, attitudes to reshape, old patterns to relearn. The way ahead was a costly way, and the season before Easter was at once a time for us to effect some of those changes, and at the same time to learn to feel good about what we had already achieved. For our church had not stood still. Like reservists on summer duty, we had begun to lose some of our flab and put on hard gospel muscle. Our attitudes were changing; so, here a little and there a little, were our practices. From time to time something happened to show us that we were indeed tough campaigners under the rule of God.

It was in this state that we approached Easter. The lectionary was now leading us through the story of Jesus en route to Jerusalem, summoning disciples to follow him even while he predicted a cross ahead.

Indeed, if we look closely at the Gospel readings, we see he had predicted not merely his own but his followers' crucifixion. There is a preaching of the cross that exempts Christians from participation. Something like, "Jesus paid it all; I'm no longer obligated." Such preaching was not our heritage. Paradoxically, Christ did carry the cross for us, and yet there is a cross for followers as well; we, too, are threatened by death row. This was plainly the case for the first disciples; I hoped my sermon would show that it was our case also, and thus help the church make gospel sense of the costly way we found ourselves traveling together.

Then he called the people to him, as well as his disciples, and said to them, "Anyone who wants to be a follower of mine must renounce self; he must take up his cross and follow me. Whoever wants to save his life will lose it, but whoever loses his life for

my sake and for the gospel's will save it. What does anyone gain
by winning the whole world at the cost of his life? What can he
give to buy his life back? If anyone is ashamed of me and my
words in this wicked and godless age, the Son of Man will be
ashamed of him, when he comes in the glory of his Father with
the holy angels."   (Mark 8:34–38)

In its long history, Palestine has often been a dangerous place.
This week is no exception. In the West Bank city of Hebron, not far
from Jerusalem, lies the traditional site of the tomb of Abraham and
Sarah, ancestors of both Arabs and Jews. A shrine marks the supposed graves, and because there are many Muslim Arabs in Hebron
and now a few Jewish immigrants as well, the shrine is divided into
two parts by a wall. One side is a mosque, the other, a synagogue.
Into the mosque, two days ago, hundreds of Arab Muslims came to
hear the sacred Koran and to kneel, face forward, in prayer. Suddenly
shots rang out, a hail of gunfire that seemed never to stop, and hundreds of the worshipers were shot, many of them murdered on the
spot. The gunman was a fanatical Jewish physician from Brooklyn,
New York, armed with an assault rifle. He resented the Arabs' presence, and sought revenge for earlier violence committed against
Jews. By his unaided action he threatened the peace negotiations
then underway, caused emergency political meetings as far away as
Washington, D.C., and rocked the fragile stability of the whole human world.

And yet how unremarkable that event was in the long history of
the land. Palestine, Israel, the land of Canaan—it has seen violence
through recorded history as great armies have marched, peoples
have migrated, and strong passions have clashed over the control of a
territory not very different from Southern California in size and climate. As it had in other centuries, this little land suffered in the
century in which Jesus lived. In his day the Romans were in control,
ruling the territory with benevolent cynicism—benevolent, insofar
as they required enough peace to enable them to collect taxes and

milk the land of its wealth and talent; cynical, inasmuch as Rome provided no justice that respected the dignity of the human occupants of the land. Wherever Rome's empire ran, the favorite method of controlling the "natives" was execution. Ghastly crucifixion was their preferred method. Political rebels trapped and arrested by Roman soldiers could expect to be stripped of all their clothing, nailed through flesh and bone to upright posts set up along a public highway, and left to die in extreme agony. It was a common sight in that countryside. Meanwhile Palestinian rebels, the New Testament's Zealots, were equally ruthless in their treatment of Romans.

We need not be surprised that under those circumstances Jesus rejected violence as a way of bringing his Father's kingdom into being. Jesus was a realist; he said that those who take the sword perish by the sword—a saying that applies all over again this week to the poor crazed Jewish physician of Qiryat Arba and to his Arab victims. What may surprise us, if we are not realists as Jesus was, is that Jesus' nonviolence did not exempt him from the same danger. When his disciples began to realize who he was, when they even (somewhat clumsily) called him "Messiah," Jesus warned them to keep the secret to themselves. Yet that led him to reveal another secret: whether they kept silent or not, there was suffering still to come, as we see in Mark 8:31:

> And he began to teach them that the Son of Man had to endure great suffering, and to be rejected (by the religious leaders); to be put to death.

Realism said that Jesus was engaged in dangerous business; realism said that the occupation army would not put up with such behavior; realism said that Rome would deal with Jesus' rebellion as Rome had dealt with all the others, in the only language Rome spoke, the language of death. He saw it coming; he warned his followers to expect it.

Every Bible reader knows that Jesus foresaw his tragic outcome. We even give a pretty name to his sad demise: Good Friday. It becomes part of a comely picture of matters religious that in today's harsh world are mainly irrelevant. Some of us go a step farther down this path of irrelevant religion: we wear pretty cross-shaped cufflinks, or cross-shaped earrings, or pretty gold crosses hung about our necks, driving the bloody reality of execution even farther back into the realm of the mythical and the otherworldly. This morning, I call you in the opposite direction. The memory of the cross at the center of our narrative signifies actual danger—for them, but also for us.

Look at what most leave out of the Jesus story: Jesus warned the disciples not only of his danger, his fate, but theirs. He called the people together and said, according to Mark 8:34:

> Anyone who wants to be a follower of mine [so there was still a choice] must take up his cross and follow me.

Exactly what did that mean? Nothing different from what the previous warning had meant: he was in danger from the occupation army—*and so were they.* He faced crucifixion; so did every one of his disciples. He was likely to end his life on one of those roadside stakes; so, if they followed him, would they.

To put it in vivid if symbolic terms, he was saying that when the end came there would be not one cross outside the city wall but thirteen crosses, one for each of the followers, and his the thirteenth. The number is symbolic, for there were more than twelve disciples; I hope it nevertheless makes the point. The road he walked was a no-man's-land; the life he lived was as risky as death row.

There are two ways for churchgoers to miss this point. One is to suppose that Jesus meant that each of the disciples would in fact die the death Romans reserved for rebellious subjects—crucifixion. Some disciples did do that; as far as we know, most did not. Paul, according to tradition, died by beheading, for he was a Roman citizen and entitled to that courtesy. Others met other fates in faraway places as they took the message everywhere.

The more common way to misunderstand, however, is embalmed in popular piety: Jesus on this view only spoke of the rather obvious fact that life has its sorrows. "Human beings are born to trouble just as sparks fly upwards" [Job 5:7 NRSV]. When we are born, we are trouble to others; as long as we live, we make trouble for ourselves; to the end of their lives, human beings suffer. They suffer colds and flu, heart trouble and cancer, kidney disease and gout. Here the Christian message reduces to stoicism, and the cross of Christ is only an instance of everybody's sorrow. If you are sick, that is your cross; if you marry unwisely, that is your cross; if your neighbors don't please you, that is your cross. Yet that is not what Jesus said. He said, "If you want to be *a follower of mine*" you must expect a cross. He did not speak of the human condition but of the cost of bearing the good news, the cost, in Palestine or anywhere else, of bringing the gospel of God into the kind of world he (and we) inhabit.

He meant to say that it would be with his followers, his true followers, as it was with him. Life was henceforth at risk for them all. Discipleship had its cost, and in a world ruled by Rome, that cost could be a cross.

How can we catch the force of this? From the confines of our comparatively safe world, can we catch the sense of danger that accompanied Christian beginnings? Danger that might mean twelve crosses on Calvary hill—or twelve hundred, if there were that many followers by then—plus a thirteenth, final cross for Jesus himself? If the disciples believed him, it surely altered their lives. Like ourselves in an earthquake season, they must have parted from one another each morning with an awareness that due to powers and forces unknown, they might not meet again. Or like prisoners on death row, they must have sensed both dread and liberty—dread of the predicted fate; liberty because they are truly free who have nothing left to lose.

In another sermon we saw the springtime of Jesus' ministry: his baptism, his breaking free of the codes and rules, the debts and customs that ground down an oppressed people. This week the story is no longer set in springtime. The long hot summer of mission has begun. Things have taken an ominous shape. He warns the disciples of dangerous days ahead. Yet there is a curious symmetry in these two seasons. Those who live on death row cease to care about some things that trouble trivial existence. Facing one consuming threat, they are unlikely to focus upon any lesser fears. So it was for Jesus and his friends. Recognizing that the God revolution in human life was final and that it required everything of them, they were liberated from minor cares.

You who know the story know that things didn't turn out as neatly as Jesus had expected. They went to Jerusalem; there was the confrontation; but at the crucial moment—but let me read it to you from Scripture, Mark 14:50:

> Then the disciples all deserted him and ran away.

All? Including blabbing Peter? Loving John? Stalwart Andrew? Earnest James? Tender Mary? Capable Martha? Yes, all. All failed, and Jesus alone was left, and then they crucified him on execution hill. So the task of keeping faith with God came down, that Friday morning, to one human being. The thirteenth cross was the only one; the others' were not even set up. He alone represented the group. He died for his supposed crime. He died alone for their betrayal of him.

That is where the idea of Christ taking our place begins. He was quite literally in the place that all the faithful might have occupied had they followed as he asked. Of course, "Christ for us" was not a new story. If we think of the Jesus story now as God's own story, we know that such substitution had happened over and over before— God had gone ahead, God had prepared a way, from the beginning. It was true when God led Israel out of Egypt and across the wilderness. God went on ahead. It was true when the prophets, Isaiah, Jeremiah, Micah, Hosea, heard the cry of God and took that cry into their own lives: the tears of God gave form to the prophetic tears. It was true when youthful Mary, selected mother-to-be, heard the angel voice and answered, "I am the Lord's servant, may it be as you have said" [Luke 1:38]. Going on before, in others' place, is the biblical way. And in Jesus it was once again true and supremely so: he died for others, too.

However, we followers are not quite left out. For there was a remarkable third day. There was a resurrection. There was by virtue of that new beginning a fresh chance at discipleship. And in the end, disciples did what Jesus had said disciples must—in resurrection power, they took up the task, took up their crosses, followed where he had led. The fact that he had gone first, holding nothing back, at last gave them the freedom to be his men and women. That story has continued through all the costly Christian centuries; that story reaches all the way to us.

❖   ❖   ❖

So what of the crosses, the first twelve crosses, here in the spring of this present year? Well, it seems not quite so dangerous to be a Christian as it was then—not if execution was the cost. There are indeed twentieth-century martyrs aplenty, massacred in Africa, imprisoned in Siberia, jailed in our own state of Georgia. In all honesty, for some present here such a time may come: give up your faith or give us your life! More likely, though, you or I will take the way of the cross in somewhat less spectacular fashion. In any case, be clear on this: the cross is not your hard luck, it is not your bad health, it is not your unemployment—*unless* that luck, that health, that loss of job is the earthly cost of your faithfulness to the way of Jesus.

The cross is exactly the cost of following Jesus in a world that does not. If you follow as he meant, it will somehow cost all that you are. That is what he asks—everything. Your life, your path, your family, your friendships, your loves, your work, your all. The old hymn said it well:

Jesus paid it all;
All to him I owe.

And if anyone says, "I cannot take on that commitment. I am not worthy," we must add the next lines as well:

Sin had left a crimson stain;
He washed it white as snow.

Our text puts it this way: there is a cross for every follower, but "whoever loses his [or her] life for my sake and for the gospel's will save it" [Mark 8:35].

Save it everlastingly.

Hard-headed Cleopas

Easter did not find our congregation as far along the road to new life as I had wanted, longed for us to be. If we were to grow, we needed newcomers passing through the doors of our church. There were plans that would attract fresh faces, but it was vital that when they came they would find us a living church, rich in faith and active in good works. Did we in fact share such a lively faith, or were we like disciples who had not yet heard the news of the empty tomb, had not yet sensed the living presence of the One whom they had known but then had lost.

Facing these circumstances, I found a likely representative of ourselves in the New Testament story. This was Cleopas, the one disciple named of the two on the road to Emmaus. Was I myself not Cleopas, wanting to be shown but determined not to be deceived? Was many another member of our congregation not Cleopas as well?

> They stood still, their faces full of sadness, and one, called Cleopas, answered, "Are you the only person staying in Jerusalem not to have heard the news of what has happened there in the last few days?" "What news?" he said. "About Jesus of Nazareth," they replied, "who, by deeds and words of power, proved himself a prophet in the sight of God and the whole people; and how our chief priests and rulers handed him over to be sentenced to death, and crucified him. But we had been hoping that he was to be the liberator of Israel. What is more, this is the third day since it happened."　　(Luke 24:17b–21)

We do not know the names of all those who followed Jesus in his mission. Some, such as James and John, Martha and Mary, appear so often in Scripture that there is some pleasure in finding a different name among the followers who walked with Jesus. Such a one is Cleopas, who appears in Luke 24 alongside another disciple whose name has not been kept. Around these two a story unfolds that tells us a good deal about the Jesus movement both then and now; I think we should hear it.

When Jesus was crucified, there was panic in the ranks of his followers. Their high hopes for the coming Rule of God were turned into sad memories. Jesus had called them, and taught them, and they had supposed that was the prelude to some grand intervention of God in history: Now at last the old promises would be fulfilled; now at last God would bring the troubles of the people to an end, drive the Romans out of the country for good, and put a king, probably Jesus himself, on Israel's throne. The new age was about to begin. It was only a matter of dealing with the existing authorities. So when Jesus set out for Jerusalem, warning that his destiny was to be suffering and death, they simply had not believed him. How could God let his Chosen One suffer?

Yet how mistaken they were! Now their dreams had indeed failed. Their Master's confrontation with the authorities had ended in his arrest and trial and execution, and the followers were scattered. At first, they lay low. But as soon as it was safe, some began to slip out of town, alone or in company. One of these refugees from the terror was Cleopas.

On the third day after the execution (the day we now call Easter, but to them, only one more lonely Sunday) this Cleopas and another set out from Jerusalem toward a village where they might find lodging for their journey without attracting undue attention to themselves. It could have been a most uneventful journey. Safely past the city walls, they felt safe enough to begin talking about what had gone wrong—arguing, and as is too often the way with followers of Jesus, perhaps blaming one another with what had happened:

"We could have jumped them, that night in the garden. There were more of us."

"But Jesus told Peter to put his weapon up. He didn't want us to fight."

"Did he want us to run away? You ran!"

"I wanted to watch where they took him. Where were you when they got to the city?"

"Where were you when they took him to Pilate?"

"Where were you when they nailed him to the cross? Were you there?"

"Were you?"

And so they quarreled as they walked, and they could have jumped out of their skins when they noticed the stranger walking just behind them. The police? A spy from the high priest? Why hadn't they been more careful?

"What are you talking about, men?" the stranger asked, with the simple good cheer of a friendly traveler. Of course, it was unsuitable to say exactly what they had been talking about, so Cleopas sighed and assumed a worldly tone. They were talking, he explained, about what the whole city had been talking about.

"Haven't you heard about the execution of Jesus of Nazareth?" (The tone is slightly condescending: "Don't you know there is a new president in Washington? Are you that out of touch?") Cleopas' strategy is clear: take up the objectivity of a bystander; then if this stranger is with the police, we'll still be safe. By his tone Cleopas could be any reporter: he is Connie Chung dramatizing the latest killing in South Central; he is Tom Brokaw reporting the bad news from Bosnia. His personal involvement is swallowed up in this smooth professional distance. Like all effective liars, Cleopas comes close to the truth only to skirt it. "Don't you know about Jesus, the much-discussed prophet? Some of us even imagined he would liberate Israel!" (This last with an ironic chuckle, glossing over the fact that Cleopas had himself been one of Jesus' committed followers. Don't let that out, for heaven's sake!) And finally Cleopas, artist in objective reporting, adds a final touch: "Some of the women" (slight condescension in tone here) "even say the tomb where they buried him is open and empty—but no one has seen the missing occupant." (Now a bit of male bonding:) "You know women."

See the irony of Luke the Evangelist. Cleopas on the evening news, Cleopas the hard-headed, Cleopas the objective, Cleopas the nondisciple (as he presents himself), Cleopas who plays the part of truth-teller, says that no one has seen the Risen One. And to whom does Mister Evening News announce this fact? Why, to the Risen One himself, the stranger on the road. Cleopas' closing sentence makes the irony emphatic: "*Him* they did not see," spoken *to him* who, as the reader knows, was the very Risen One in person.

The Jewish philosopher Martin Buber thinks such irony is built into every attempted human conversation about God. For God, he says, is the One who can never be expressed, but only addressed; that is, we can only talk *with* God, never merely *about* him. To attempt to talk objectively of God is for Buber necessarily comical: scholars sitting about the table like so many college sophomores discussing whether God exists, while God listens (standing in a corner, perhaps, since no one offers God a seat). Perhaps God waits to find the outcome of the argument? Will the sophomores declare God extinct, this time? Be wary when anyone speaks thus of God.

What has this comic irony to do with us? The knowledgeable Cleopas explains to the risen Christ what has been happening in Jerusalem. I think this Cleopas is ourselves. We watch the news with Dan Rather, or MacNeil and Lehrer, or some other expert of the screen or the papers or the radio, and from this we think we find out what is going on. Thus our world is what it is because we hear what we hear. In that newscaster world there is hatred and envy, lust and lies; in it power matters and the strong always prevail. Sometimes Jesus of Nazareth and his followers drift into this picture. We Christians are only at the margins, on the inconsequential church page. Or very occasionally we are at the center, when a Billy Graham or a Pope John Paul or some mitered Russian bishop or miscreant televangelist briefly impinges upon the great world, the "real" world, of ships and shoes and cabbages. When Jesus and his people do enter that picture, the world sees us only as transient figures, evanescent extras hired for a day and soon to go, and so we see ourselves. Cleopas, stand-in for ourselves, can see the gospel in this world's perspective and discount it as the world discounts us. Jesus is dead; the world knows that. The empty tomb is an unconfirmed bit of local gossip; we had hoped it might be otherwise, but we were mistaken.

There were, of course, a few clues that might have changed Cleopas' mind. In the first place, there was *the fellowship of gathering for prayer.* Back in Jerusalem, disciples who were not fleeing had gathered to pray, and in that gathering the risen Christ himself would shortly appear. Cleopas ought not to have been hiking out of town that Sunday; he ought to have been with the other disciples. It was a lesson to remember, later on.

Another disturbing clue was *the sense of Scripture.* Cleopas had followed Jesus with all the rest, and if you yourself will go through this Gospel of Luke with a green pencil and mark the places where the Old Testament is quoted and explained, you will see that one of Jesus' main tasks had been to teach followers to read him by learning to read that Book. In its reference, the Bible was God's long story with Israel; in its thrust, it was a story that climaxed in himself. Had Cleopas only learned to read the Bible, he might have read the evening news with different eyes. Instead, his Sunday school teacher, the risen Christ, had to track him down on the highway to call his attention to lessons already taught. Why didn't Cleopas get it? The Risen One has a short explanation: "How *dull* you are," he says [Luke 24:25].

Not least among overlooked clues, Cleopas had forgotten *the road, the way.* He took the road that led to a country village, but he forgot the road Jesus had shown him: that true road leads in the other direction. The road is Jesus' kingdom way; it leads toward the cross, not away from it. Many people today try to understand Christianity as if it were an insurance policy, a chain-link fence to keep out trouble, an armed guard patrol service to keep life's ills away forever. Christian faith is none of these things. Following Jesus will get you *into* trouble, not out of it, but this is holy trouble, trouble that will transform your life into a song of sacrificial love. Cleopas had known that, once, or he could not have followed Jesus. Now he forgot; hence he could not see Jesus on the road.

❖ ❖ ❖

I must skip on to the end of the story. It is a happy ending. In it, hard-headed Cleopas and his companion come to see the world for what it is. At last they recognize the Stranger, the Risen One. It might have happened, I think, if the three of them had found a Samaritan traveler wounded and lying beside the road. Then, doubtless, the Stranger would have stopped, and offered first aid, and put the wounded one on his own back if need be, and brought him safely to the inn. In such conduct, we recognize the Christ; in such deeds, we know this world's last reality; in such acts of love we discover the God of love.

Or the happy ending might have come (and in fact it almost did!) as Cleopas and his companion listened to the Stranger explaining the whole message of the whole Bible. God, who had been faithful in Genesis and Exodus to Abraham and Moses, has been faithful once more, this time at Passover in Jerusalem. Cleopas might have rediscovered in Isaiah the summons of a holy God who says (Isaiah 58:7):

> *Is {true religion} not sharing your food with the hungry,*
> *taking the homeless poor into your house,*
> *clothing the naked when you meet them,*
> *and never evading a duty to your kinsfolk?*

Thus from their Sunday school lesson that Easter day these traveling church members might have understood God's long purposes fulfilled in Jesus. In fact, they said later, their hearts had indeed been "on fire when he explained to them in the whole of scripture the things that referred to himself" [Luke 24:32].

In actual fact the breakthrough came in none of those ways. It finally came when with the Stranger these disciples turned in to the inn, sat down at table, and as the time came for prayer and the breaking of bread, the Scripture says,

> He took bread and said the blessing; he broke the bread, and offered it to them. Then their eyes were opened, and they recognized him.   [Luke 24:30–31]

And with him risen, there was a new world. Now Connie Chung could never satisfy; now Tom Brokaw, or the *Jerusalem Post,* or the whole blinded world itself could never truly explain the news, for the real news, the really new, was in Christ Jesus, and once again *they knew him.*

God

The hard work many congregants had expended during the year began to bear fruit. Visitors did now attend our church, and some were led into full membership. With a certain amount of shifting and heaving, the new Bible study classes took shape, and some of them, as expected, attracted members on their own. Even more encouraging to me was the hunger many began to display for more Bible teaching. Our ministry of Christian service or witness held firm as well, thanks to many helpers, many hands. And the shape of Christian worship in our congregation began to offer a happy alternative to the folksy banality that characterized so many churches like ours.

A new project, to be called "Quest," engaged us next. We would blanket our church's area (several square miles) with fliers advertising a "Christian Quest," a kind of combination singing school, mission, revival meeting, newcomers class, and prayer workshop on weekday evenings. Three skilled leaders would lead us in a week of evening meetings in the coming June. One leader would conduct a kind of music school, a program of participatory Christian singing each evening; another would guide us into skills of prayer; a third (I myself would be the third leader) would teach the elementary doctrines of Christian faith. We envisioned Quest as a meeting that could be easily attended by those who so far found the regular Sunday service too intimidating or too remote from their own lives.

Meantime, the most promising news of all was that our search committee had found a highly qualified candidate who might be willing to come to our congregation as pastor. A graduate of the very seminary where my wife and I taught and a long-time member of our denomination, the new candidate seemed to have everything. And she was a woman! Hooray!

With these plans in place, I felt free to devote at least some sermons to my own special skills in doctrine. This sermon, preached on Trinity Sunday (next after Pentecost) is an example. It is not an easy sermon—but then, neither is the doctrine it unfolds. One such sermon per year is doubtless enough!

> The Spirit of God affirms to our spirit that we are God's chil-
> dren; and if children, then heirs, heirs of God and fellow-heirs
> with Christ; but we must share his sufferings if we are also to
> share his glory.   (Rom. 8:16–17)

I am always amazed, and often delighted, by those of our members who Sunday by Sunday present "Children's Time" in our service. It is one of the chief elements of our worship, and I notice that adults are often more eager to hear the children's message than they are to hear the grown-up sermon from this pulpit. Perhaps we sense that when it comes to God and faith we are all little children. You may be thankful, though, that there is this difference between their sermon and ours: beginning with questions is not the practice when we come to the big folks' sermon. If it were, there might be long silences, much longer than our silent prayers. Take the question, "Who is God?" Who wants to answer? Or this one: "How many Gods are there?" One, surely. Yet we believe God the Creator to be God? Yes. And we believe the risen Lord Jesus Christ to be God the Word? Yes. And we believe God who is Holy Spirit to be God? Yes, so we teach. God the Father, God the Word, God the Holy Spirit? Well, yes. So how many Gods are there? Silence.

Now such silence is not wrong. To speak of God is to speak of the mystery that surrounds our life. Better reverent silence than over-confident blabbing. God, said the Jewish thinker Martin Buber, is the one who is always to be addressed, never expressed; that is, we are right to talk to God (and to listen for God), but we are too bold if we set out to explain God or define God. Unless here we become as little children, finite and frail in face of the Eternal, we risk presumption and blasphemy. Those who pronounce about God in a loud voice (or write about God in smooth self-assurance) are the real blasphemers; they take God's name in vain. Flee from such teachers as you would avoid drifting poison gas.

Yet today is Trinity Sunday, and custom says your preacher will speak of one God who is Father and Son and Spirit, God triune or three-in-one. This is the God we acknowledge in our practice of baptism, this is the God we invoke whenever we pray in Jesus' name though we do not pray in saints' names or in our own precious names, the God we acknowledge in hand and mouth at eucharist and Love Feast. This is the triune God of the apostolic benediction:

The grace of the Lord Jesus Christ,
and the love of God,
and the fellowship of the Holy Spirit,
be with you all.

{2 Cor. 13:14}.

So it is my job to speak to you about the trinity or threeness of the one God. What, in heaven's name, am I to say?

Perhaps we can take a first step forward by asking, Where is God? If this were Children's Time, someone might answer, "In heaven." And that would be quite right. This is how you are to pray, says Jesus, and then begins, "Our Father in heaven" [Matt. 6:9]. Heaven is God's home or abode, for God according to Scripture is the "maker of heaven and earth" [Ps. 124:8]. Do we know what heaven is? In fact, we do not yet fully know what earth is. If we stray off the sidewalk where there is no grass, we are walking on earth. Yet earth is more—it is the grass as well, and the mountains; it is the sidewalk and the waterways; it is the oceans, the continents, the round globe entire.

Yet it is still more: earth is all that is earthy. The *New York Times* last Thursday [May 26, 1994] reported that the Hubble telescope (which one of our members helped to machine at Caltech's Jet Propulsion Laboratory) has observed a black hole near the center of galaxy M87, fifty million light-years away, a black hole whose diameter alone is five hundred light-years. Now in the language of Scripture as we learn to read it today, that black hole is not part of heaven but part of earth; it is not the home of God but only a part of our own vast home. We are in earth, in the cosmos; God is in heaven. "Heaven," says theologian Karl Barth, "is the creation inconceivable to [human beings]; earth is the creation conceivable to [us]." The ancient creeds spoke of "things visible and invisible." What the Hubble can see, what the astronomer or philosopher can conceive, what the creature can imagine—that is still the cosmos, still of the earth, earthy.

Our best scientific minds, our Einsteins, our Hubbles, are stretched to conceive such a cosmos—this is what the psalmist denotes as earth. What is the shape of the universe? How can it have edges? What is its age, its extent, its future? How little we know! How, then, can we go on to think of heaven, the abode of God? The answer is that we cannot, and that is just the point. When our capacity to deal with space-time is exhausted, when science, art, morality, religion have had their say and at last fall silent, when every human limit has been passed—there the abode of God begins: "Our Father who art in heaven."

Yet just here the wonder of biblical faith begins. The God of heaven, the God who is Other, the transcendent One who dwells in light unapproachable: Scripture names this One by the humble name "Father," and we sing hymns to celebrate his tenderness and gentle love:

> *Fatherlike he tends and spares us;*
> *Well our feeble frame he knows. . . .*

How dare we? By what right can we treat the ineffable God as a gentle, loving parent; with what insolence speak of the Lord of glory as a shepherd, with what chutzpah pray for the kingdom of heaven to come *on earth*?

The answer, though, is that it is the character of this very God to draw near the creature, to come to us who can find no way to him. The one who made the stars made us, and would not leave us to ourselves. God is not only in the heaven of heavens but appears within the human story; not only Lord of history but Lord within history, the Maker as a thing made; the God without sorrow as a sorrowing child of woman, the Father of lights as one upon whom darkness will finally fall. Immanuel. God with us.

You mean to say, some critic cries, that Jesus was God! And is shocked by such ignorance, such blasphemy. Now if anyone does say Jesus was God, we have to think who speaks before we respond. If it is a little child, perhaps we gently correct her or him: "Jesus was God's best friend," we say, "a better friend than any other ever could be." That moves in the right direction, without making of God an earthly demon or of Jesus a masquerading pretense at human life. Or if it is an adolescent who asks, "Is Jesus God?" perhaps we offer the old churchly image of two natures in the one Christ, a divine nature and a human one as well, yet only one person of two natures consisting. That explanation served thought for quite a few centuries. And yet again, if the one who says "Jesus was God" is a wise and mature Christian, one who has grown old, secure in the faith and perhaps already longing for the heavenly home, we may simply say yes in reply, for that one has outgrown all the complexities of theology and sees things, as a great artist might, quite simply and directly. "The only God I expect to see in heaven," my old theology teacher Walter T. Conner used to say, "is the God I will see when I finally look into the face of Jesus Christ."

Indeed, how could it be otherwise? God is not a creature, and so the forms under which God is perceived must be those that suggest, that convey, the divine reality that (as forms alone) they could not be. Jesus was and remains truly and fully human: Jesus tells us what human life must be. Yet in his way of being human we meet and are mastered by the very life of God who is God—not another God, not a second God, but the one, the only God there is.

Notice, too, the earlier lesson repeated: If Jesus shows us what God is like in history, we therefore learn from him what God means history to be—not the history of wars, of hatred, of evil, of destruction, but the quiet history that bears the suffering of the world without complaint and shows the way to the healing of the present world, shows its true beauty, shows it the way of peace.

Where is God? It seems we have answered. God is God above all, *in heaven,* utterly different from what we can conceive, and nonetheless the loving Parent who tends and feeds us. We know it is so, for God is also God the Word; God is God *in history.* Israel's story climaxes in the character we call Jesus the Christ, who demands of us loyalty that must be yielded to God but to no other. For the curious, the speculative, the mere thinker, we have said enough: God is far and God is near, God above us and yet facing us. We are not atheists, for we know God as loving Father; we are not idolaters, for the only earthly God we know is this crucified and risen Son who is one with God: "I and my Father are one" [John 10:30].

Yes, but so far we still have not reached Christian ground, for all this seems to leave ourselves untouched. Christianity only begins when a third movement occurs, so that God is known not only in heaven and in history, but *in the fellowship* itself. The earliest disciples knew God "the Father"; had not Jesus taught them to pray "Our Abba in heaven"? After he was risen, they recognized that they had also known God in Jesus their Master; it was Thomas who put this into words, crying, "My Lord and my God" [John 20:28]. But something was yet to occur.

Last week we celebrated Pentecost—the tongues as of flame, the unfamiliar speech, the ecstatic glory of outpoured Spirit. Yet Scripture tells other, quieter stories of the Spirit-gift: of the risen Christ Jesus breathing upon the disciples and saying "receive the Spirit" [John 20:19–23]; of baptisms where the Spirit baptized as well [Acts 10:47]; of missionaries who "in the Spirit" crossed seas, grew churches, faced persecution, gave their witness. In all these stories, two themes recur: where Christ is preached, Spirit winds blow; where the Spirit enters, Christ is hailed as Lord. In this light we interpret today's text, Romans 8:16–17:

> The Spirit of God affirms to our spirit that we are God's chil-
> dren, . . . heirs of God and fellow-heirs with Christ.

Here is the place of fellowship. Christians do not teach that a few special adepts only are touched by God; rather the Apostle says that as members of the fellowship, *all* have the gift. There is no way to be a sister or a brother here save by being a regular member of this family. The good news this church has to offer is this: there is family here, and family, if you will have it, for you. You don't have to face your troubles alone; you don't have to bear your guilt alone; you don't have to face the failures of your earthly family alone; for here, as the Spirit-gift from God, is family for you. We pray together; we learn together; together we minister to a hurting world. Do you want to pray? Do you want to learn? Do you want to help others? Then God, it may be, is saying to you, be strangers no more, but members of this family.

Suppose you had to lead Children's Time on Trinity Sunday. And suppose you had begun by asking, where *is* God? *In heaven?* That answer is true, and it matters, because we pray that earth shall become like heaven. God is the Almighty Creator, but a Creator who, fatherlike, draws near us. The concrete evidence of that nearness is Jesus. Hence, "Where is God?" has for Christians a second answer: God is *where Jesus is,* healing the sick, saving the lost, guiding the perplexed, giving his life for us. In Jesus—that is where God is. Yet we have precocious children here, and quite likely one will answer, God is *right here.* And that would be the last, best truth: God is here because here is the Christian community, and God is Spirit for us in this place. So how many Gods are there? Only one, only one. For Spirit and Word and Father are one God, simply one, known to us in these three ways, but known as God, that One.

Dreaming

After the church began to reckon that its troubles could be surmounted, there was for a time the idea that I might continue as interim pastor, or even as pastor, yet with a reduced workload that would require an associate pastor who would eventually take over the whole task. The pastoral search committee considered that possibility. But at that time they found no one who filled the bill, and meantime the sheer fatigue of weekly sermon preparation coupled with the other emergency duties, together with confronting the unfulfilled need for organizational overhaul, led me to urge that a regular pastor be called. A young minister was found who received the unanimous call from the congregation. That (in our polity) constituted her election. She accepted; the thing was done!

There were delays in putting the new pastor in place, delays that I found very uncomfortable as I could see behind-the-scenes work that urgently needed doing; yet finally, at summer's end, far into Pentecost season, the awaited arrival day for the new minister was set, and at last I had a "last sermon" to preach. I decided to evoke again the Pentecostal setting.

This sermon sprang from texts from two parts of the Bible, Old and New. It is surely a great mistake to confuse the regular reading of Scripture from both testaments in worship with the preacher's necessary task of selecting one preaching text, which normally must come from one reading or the other, or from some third passage, if the resultant sermon is to possess unity. This time seemed to me an exception, and I print both texts in full here.

Perhaps it is true that older folk typically dream of the past, while the young see visions of the future; certainly for the one life is beginning as for the other it ends. And most of our members were in the older category. Yet I could not exclude them from the visionary, the future-seeing, the reshaping, that was our mission. It was a time of optimism in the congre-

gation, a time of hope. This sermon must reflect and intensify that hope focused upon the gospel, the good news yet to come.

> *After this I shall pour out my spirit on all mankind;*
> *your sons and daughters will prophesy,*
> *your old men will dream dreams*
> *and your young men see visions.*
> *I shall pour out my spirit in those days*
> *even on slaves and slave-girls.*
> *I shall set portents in the sky and on earth,*
> *blood and fire and columns of smoke.*
> *The sun will be turned to darkness*
> *and the moon to blood*
> *before the coming of the great and terrible day of the* LORD.
> *Then everyone who invokes the* LORD's *name will be saved.*
> (*Joel 2:28–32a*)

In the last days, says God, I will pour out my Spirit on all mankind; and your sons and daughters shall prophesy; your young men shall see visions, and your old men shall dream dreams. Yes, on my servants and my handmaids I will pour out my Spirit in those days, and they shall prophesy. I will show portents in the sky above, and signs on the earth below—blood and fire and a pall of smoke. The sun shall be turned to darkness, and the moon to blood, before that great, resplendent day, the day of the LORD, shall come. Everyone who calls on the name of the LORD on that day shall be saved. (Acts 2:17–21)

Even dogs dream! Watching their closed eyes, their twitching bodies, we suspect they dream of doggy delights of food and fun and a Master's fondling hand. About our own dreams there is still less doubt: dream memories linger when we wake, and sometimes—as in the case of nightmares—these seem more real than waking life. Dreams are real in any case.

Sigmund Freud, the founder of psychoanalysis, uncovered in remembered and half-remembered dreams an avenue of access to another mental system lurking within the human psyche. In the dream world our elemental selves are revealed, more "It" than "I." There we act out our lusts and disclose our fears. Dreams tell us what we would be if we remained in the primal state, polymorphously perverse, dogs indeed, without masters.

For Freud's pupil Carl Jung, dreams were closer still to waking reality; like memories and reflections (daydreams, we call these last), Jung's dreams showed the link of the self with a wider psychic world, a collective unconscious in which each participates in racial memories older than civilization.

For the Bible, though, neither Freud nor Jung is sufficiently radical. For Scripture, dreams are access, not merely into the primal depths of selfhood, individual or communal, but into the deep mystery of life lived under the eyes of God. The Pharaoh dreams, and Joseph interprets; Nebuchadnezzar dreams, and Daniel both remembers his dream and interprets it for him—Freuds before Freud, Jungs before Jung, these ancient men of God.

In the old order, interpreters of dream were the selected few, the rare ones to whom people turned for insight and guidance. Where was God leading? What did the future hold? The answer lay with God's forth-tellers, the *nabhi,* a chosen few with the gift of prophetic insight, able to see the true meaning of things, able, therefore, to see how life was bound to come out. Yet reserving prophetic sight to the few was a temporary matter: the time was coming, said the prophetic books, when all God's children would prophesy, all would share the dream gifts of the coming age.

One such prophecy about the flourishing of prophecy is found in the book of Joel, dated around 400 B.C. Seeing the judgment of God issue in repentance and renewal, Joel declared that God was about to

pour out my spirit [God's spirit] on all mankind.   (Joel 2:28f.)

Now without doubt that vision was fulfilled in Joel's own day. I don't doubt that the Spirit of God was poured out on old Jews, young Jews, earnest Jews, hopeful Jews of Joel's own era, sending them back to read his and other prophetic books, filling the synagogues of Joel's time with seekers and learners, shaping a people free from foreign domination, forming a people who could be bearers of God's truth not only in the Jerusalem temple but in synagogues of God-worshipers wherever in the Jewish diaspora learning and devotion spread.

The wonderful thing about the *good* news the Bible tells is this: it never happens only once. Time went by, and Jesus was born—Jesus who knew the prophets, Jesus who interpreted the law, Jesus who brought God's Rule to earth anew. You know the story—how he lived as never any lived, and spoke as never any spoke, and yet the enemies came, accused him of evil, took him away, tried him as a criminal, executed him on a Roman cross—on the cross, that monument to the high civilization of the classical world. Jesus was dead; God had failed.

Yet as we know for sure, the story did not end there. There was a third day and a mysterious missing body; there were uncanny visits from a Risen Lord; the story would continue; Christ was risen; hallelujah! And now, as it had before, as it would again, that old story took shape once more: God's Spirit was poured out afresh. We call this occasion Pentecost. The new that came in Christ was not to be limited to one human life, to Mary's baby, Joseph's son. The new was for all who would hear, all who would receive, all who would let the baptismal waters close over them, covering their bodies, healing their souls. Simon Peter said it clearly enough on Pentecost day: These new believers are not barflies, carousers, drunken fools; they are fools for Christ, carousers in the Spirit, drunkards on the new wine of the Spirit of God. God has acted again, just as Joel said: *this is that!* [Acts of the Apostles 2:16, King James Version]. And so the movement was on; the news was spread: God is with us; earth shall again be fair.

That movement has come to us also. We have gone through some dark days in our church. In our past there have been divisions; there have been misunderstandings; there have been seasons of unfaithfulness. I believe in judgment; as I see it, we have been judged by God for our failures, and some of the pain we have endured as a people has been punishment for our failure to hear God's persistent call to us. Enough of that now. That is a closed matter; it belongs to a past day. This is Pentecost season; we see God's promises kept again: "I will pour out my Spirit upon all flesh."

Yet someone may challenge me. Someone may say, "I do not see the hand of God in this church. I do not believe God is with us. I see here only human strength and human weakness; nothing more." Well, such a critic is not all wrong or merely wrong; there is human strength here, and human weakness as well. Who could be more conscious of that weakness than I? During the months of this interim I found my own strength insufficient, found it harder and harder as the long months went by to provide the sermon every week, keep up the effort to structure our work afresh, hold together God's restless flock. Where was God in that deficiency of mine? Well, if I had not grown weak, how would God have led us on to the young pastor we have found? Three times I came to you, once to the church assembled in February to ask for an assistant pastor, once to the commission on ministry to ask for an administrative secretary, again to the search committee in May to ask that you find not a helper but a replacement able to take up my work. And by the grace of God (as I believe) the last has happened in the unanimous call you extended to one who comes next Sunday to become pastor here.

God is in our midst, answering our prayers, leading the sheep, and God promises that where the Spirit is, the young folk will see visions and the old folk will dream dreams. Do our old folk dream dreams? Not just doggy dreams of food and fun and no leashes ever again, but spiritual dreams, high dreams of God's future? Are you thirty-five or over, half your life already lived? Then I put the question to you who are (by that measure) already old: Are you dreaming great dreams?

Let one who is old by that and several other standards share a dream or two with you. I dream of our church moving forward to do some things that no other church in our city or round about is able to do. I have a dream that one day, not too far in the future, we will discover the unique capacity of our church to minister to many mature folk, some of whom will surely become members of our church. How will we minister to the mature? Why, by doing what we do already: We will feed them. Our Wednesday nights are famous. Here people come who want to see friends, who do not want to eat alone, who yearn for friendship and good food. What if we called our Wednesday meal the *agape feast* (copying the ancient church); what if we gradually extended its days of operation, a little more each year, until developing from our present summer-only pattern we came to have a Wednesday feast year-round? What if we made it a regular time when grown-up folk can together realize the love of Jesus? I have that dream.

Again, I dream of a time when our weekly prayer, this service of worship on Sunday morning, will draw many of these same seniors to return to hear the word of God, be bathed in baptismal waters (too many of our dear friends remain unbaptized, not washed in the blood of the Lamb), and then be fed with the spiritual food of Christ's body and blood at the Lord's table set here week by week. I dream that someday this meetingroom space will be remodeled so that, like our present chapel, it can draw us together in a spiritual architecture as yet undrawn, so that we can see one another's faces when we meet (rather than the backs of one another's necks), so that we can hear without artificial help, and so that great music will pour from the chest of each brother and sister and from our instruments as well, and so that we will pray great prayers, and this place where we meet will be shaken. I have that dream.

There is more to my dream, but now I must speak differently. For the Scripture says that your old will dream dreams, but that your young will see visions. What about that? Where are these young to come from, and how are they to come here, and what visions will they see? Well, the answer to the first is easy: when the seniors begin to gather and grow in the power of the Spirit, then we will find that they are parents and uncles and aunts and grandparents, so of course they will have daughters and sons and nephews and nieces and grandsons and granddaughters and friends of nephews and parents of grandchildren and on and on. When the seniors come, when the Spirit is poured out on the old, then (and in our case, only then) will the juniors come as well. So it is today; so it will be then.

What visions will they see? Let us be clear about this. We are talking of God's gift to the young. We are talking of the Spirit, not of human wishes or tastes—of the pouring out of the Spirit of God. You and I cannot know what the Spirit will give, but we can be sure that God's Spirit is not a Spirit of division, not a Spirit who will set young against old, not a Spirit of antagonism to our heritage, not a Spirit of bad taste or ugliness or discord. God who has led us all this way is not going to cast us off tomorrow.

What will they see, then, these young who see visions? We do not know, but we have the pages of Scripture before us, so we can surmise. Acts 2:18–20:

> I will pour out my Spirit in those days, and they shall prophesy.
> I will show portents in the sky above, and signs on the earth
> below—blood and fire and a pall of smoke. The sun shall be
> turned to darkness, and the moon to blood, before that great,
> resplendent day, the day of the Lord, shall come.

No one of Anabaptist heritage, baptist heritage, no child of this church, can read that passage without recalling that the vision is never all sugar and cream. This is apocalyptic language. It speaks of suffering saints, of ardors still unknown. It says that when the followers of the crucified stand with him alongside the poor, when they are faithful to the way of Jesus, when they are obedient to God in this present age, there is a price to pay. What that price is, when it will come, we cannot now foretell, but we know that to be a disciple is to take up such a cross. Even our dreams must be lived out by the seers of our vision, the young who will come after us.

It is time to sum up. Why are there dreams? The answer is that dreams make human life whole. Deprived of sleep we perish, and in part that is because then we cannot dream. Deprived of prophetic dreams, the church withers: our old must dream dreams and our young see visions if we are to be the faithful church, the witnessing church, the church of Jesus Christ. Now I step down from this pulpit never to return *in this role,* yet be sure of this: I shall not cease to dream. Nor must we, nor must we, if the church is to be the church, and the Spirit of God preside in this place.

Afterword

The end is the beginning. An interim pastorate is at best but an interlude in the life of any church. I knew that references to "the previous pastor" would never mean myself, but would only refer to the one whose unhappy departure had brought our recent troubles to the boil. The new pastor (it was unanimously hoped) would be the one to take us past all our troubles—or at least all but that true trouble that is the way of the cross. I was an in-between, neither the previous pastor nor the "next pastor." And that suited me well enough. Yet what of the things happily achieved during the interim year? Would they, too, be discarded in a new beginning?

The Free Church is typically short of institutional means to make its internal reforms stick. Word, worship, and witness often go adrift in a weather of uncertainties. Like a boat with no keel, this model of the church of Jesus Christ is uncomfortably vulnerable to swift, unplanned changes of current. The stability of such congregations depends either upon the lasting influence of some towering personality (usually a beloved pastor of long tenure), or upon policies hammered into working documents along with the will to abide by them, or upon practices in themselves so powerful and so enduring that they could not be overturned, come wind come weather. The new directions I had urged had to depend upon this third sort of stabilizing force: upon our thirst for the great gospel signs, aroused by their explication, stimulated by their frequent, happy practice.

Though it had been a long (and often a weary) year for this head-in-the-clouds professor, that was a very short period of time in which to form enduring good habits in the church—or to reform bad ones. This was so, even if the good habits better fulfilled our historic baptist mission.

So how did it all come out, in this case? Like the readers of *Catriona* or *Huckleberry Finn,* my readers, and I, too, want to know what happened to the characters in this book after the end of the book.

A visitor to the little congregation today would find much that is continuous with the patterns of its interim year as we have seen them here. One would also find some healthy new ventures being launched. And yet some things that had seemed firm achievements of the interim year may have slipped away unnoticed. Alas, it would be invidious to name these, for to do so here would seem only to proffer unseemly afterthoughts. Perhaps, though, even unlabeled they serve to remind us that human life, including human life lived in gospel perspective, is forever frail and insecure.

How much do they matter, these lost gains? That remains unclear, for it is really too soon to say. Will this congregation on trial continue upon its journey well begun into gospel life and health? I hope so—with what seems an inordinate, lover's hope, I hope so. Or was the interim only to have been a period of remission in an ultimately fatal illness? Concretely, is baptism still to be the focus of the worldly, outward-looking orientation demanded by the gospel? Is this church still to be troubled, healthily troubled, because the "distinguished disadvantaged" in our valley and our city are not yet being reached by our faltering evangelism? Is the pattern of our worship still to be truly catholic, though truly baptist as well?

In particular, will the traditional Love Feast, with its significant, climactic bread and cup, and the more frequent (and more common) eucharist whose focus is the same, again give shape to our shared community life? Shape to our teaching? Shape to our witness? Shape, formative shape, to our weekly worship? Shall we thus again and again offer in that bread and that cup the living prayer of our enduring fellowship?

And (to return to this volume's preoccupation) is prophetic preaching—with its amazing Janus power to face both outward and inward, both toward the world and toward the church, both to God and to the creature—still to be our ceaseless sign from God?

Certainly the issue is in doubt. Once again there is fog ahead for the church. Once again—yet this time, as I see them dimly through the fog, gospel lights do gleam. There is hope. And (according to the Apostle—Romans 8:24), it is with such hope that in this present age we are saved.

BOOKLIST

Abbott, Edwin Abbott. *Flatland: A Romance of Many Dimensions*. London: Seeley and Co., 1884.

Barth, Karl. *Dogmatics in Outline*. London: SCM, 1949.

Begbie, Harold. *Twice Born Men*. New York: Revell, 1909.

Braght, Thieleman van. *Martyrs Mirror*. Scottdale, Pa.: Herald Press, 1979.

Buber, Martin. *I and Thou*. New York: Scribner's, 1970.

Bunyan, John. *Grace Abounding, in The Pilgrim's Progress and Grace Abounding*. Edited by James Thorpe. New York: Houghton Mifflin, 1969.

Carroll, Jackson W., ed. *Small Churches Are Beautiful*. New York: Harper and Row, 1977.

Douglas, Mary. *Purity and Danger*. London: Routledge and Kegan Paul, 1978.

Lewis, C. S. *The Four Loves*. New York: Harcourt Brace, 1960.

McClendon, James. Wm., Jr. *Biography as Theology*. Valley Forge, Pa.: Trinity Press International, 1990.

———. *Ethics*. Vol. 1 of *Systematic Theology*. Nashville: Abingdon, 1986.

———. *Doctrine*. Vol. 2 of *Systematic Theology*. Nashville: Abingdon, 1994.

———. *Conversations*. Vol. 3 of *Systematic Theology*. Nashville: Abingdon, forthcoming.

McClendon, James Wm., Jr., and James M. Smith. *Convictions: Defusing Religious Relativism*. Valley Forge, Pa.: Trinity Press International, 1994.

McPhee, John. *The Control of Nature*. New York: Farrar, Straus, and Giroux, 1988.

Myers, Ched. *Binding the Strong Man*. Maryknoll, N.Y.: Orbis, 1988.

Ray, David R. *The Big Small Church Book.* Cleveland: The Pilgrim Press, 1992.

Underhill, Evelyn. *Worship.* New York: Harper and Bros., 1937.

Van Bracht, Thielemann J. *Martyrs Mirror.* Scottdale, Pa.: Herald Press, 1979 (1st ed. 1660).

SCRIPTURE INDEX

INDEX OF AUTHORS CITED